EMPTY WORDS

EMPTY WORDS

Writings '73–'78 by *John Cage*

WESLEYAN UNIVERSITY PRESS *Middletown, Connecticut*

Library of Congress Cataloging in Publication Data

Cage, John.
    Empty words.

    1. Music—Addresses, essays, lectures. 2. Music—History and criticism—20th century. I. Title.
ML60.C12   780′.8   78-27212
ISBN 0-8195-5032-9

Manufactured in the United States of America
FIRST EDITION

To the students in the school
from which we'll never graduate

Contents

Recently I was a houseguest in Paris. At breakfast I was talking with another guest in the same home, a lady from Australia. In response to a newsreport, I said, "Why? Why did it happen?" The lady from Melbourne said, "That is a question for which there is no longer an answer."

I am an optimist. That is my raison d'être. But by the news each day I've been in a sense made dumb. In 1973 I began another installment of my *Diary: How to Improve the World (You Will Only Make Matters Worse)*: it remains unfinished.

Foreword

Buckminster Fuller too from prophet of Utopia has changed to Jeremiah. He now gives us eight to ten years to make essential changes in human behaviour.

Perhaps all of us are needlessly shocked and alarmed. A subtle but radical change may be taking place which only superficially deprives us of our wits, which fundamentally is altering for the good mankind's condition. Let us hope so. Wishful thinking?

EMPTY WORDS

When in 1975 Richard Coulter of the Canadian Broadcasting Corporation offered me a commission to write a piece of music to celebrate the American Bicentennial, I automatically accepted because the invitation came from outside the United States. He suggested that I base it on texts of Benjamin Franklin. I got a copy of *Poor Richard's Almanac* but shortly put it aside, returning to the writings of Thoreau, the *Essay on Civil Disobedience*, the *Journal*, and *Walden*.

[Recently, in the course of preparing a European tour, June 1978, with Grete Sultan and Paul Zukofsky, during which I would sometimes read an excerpt from *Empty Words* Part III, I found that an otherwise cultivated Swiss thought Thoreau was French, didn't know he was an American, let alone know anything about his work. I therefore wrote the following program note:

Henry David Thoreau (1817–1862) lived in Concord, Massachusetts. For two years he lived alone in the woods, two miles from town, by the side of Walden Pond. He built his

Preface to "Lecture on the Weather"

home and grew his food, and each Sunday walked back to Concord to have dinner with his mother and father and other relatives or friends. He is the inventor of the pencil (he was the first person to put a piece of lead down the center of a piece of wood). He wrote many books including a *Journal* of fourteen volumes (two million words). His *Essay on Civil Disobedience* inspired Gandhi in his work of changing India, and Martin Luther King, Jr., in his use of nonviolence as a means of revolution. No greater American has lived than Thoreau. Emerson called him a speaker and actor of the truth. Other great men have vision. Thoreau had none. Each day his eyes and ears were open and empty to see and hear the world he lived in. Music, he said, is continuous; only listening is intermittent. He did have a question: Is life worth living? *Walden* is his detailed and affirmative reply.]

Subjecting Thoreau's writings to *I Ching* chance operations to obtain collage texts, I prepared parts for twelve speaker-vocalists (or -instrumentalists), stating my preference that they be American men who had become Canadian citizens. Along with these parts go recordings by Maryanne Amacher of breeze, rain, and finally thunder and in the last (thunder) section a film by Luis Frangella representing lightning by means of briefly projected negatives of Thoreau's drawings. Before a performance of *Lecture on the Weather*, the following text is read as a Preface.

The first thing I thought of doing in relation to this work was to find an anthology of American aspirational thought and subject it to chance operations. I thought the resultant complex would help to change our present intellectual climate. I called up Dover and asked whether they published such an anthology. They didn't. I called a part of Columbia University concerned with American History and asked about aspirational thought. They knew nothing about it. I called the Information Desk of the New York Public Library at 42nd Street. The man who answered said: You may think I'm not serious, but I am; if you're interested in aspiration, go to the Children's Library on 52nd Street. I did. I found that anthologies for children are written by adults: they are what adults think are good for children. The thickest one was edited by Commager (*Documents of American History*). It is a collection of legal judgments, presidential reports, congressional speeches. I began to realize that what is called balance between the branches of our government is not balance at all: all the branches of our government are occupied by lawyers.

Of all professions the law is the least concerned with aspiration. It is concerned with precedent, not with discovery, with what was witnessed at one time in one place, and not with vision and intuition. When the law is corrupt, it is corrupt because it concentrates its energy on protecting the rich from the poor. Justice is out of the question. That is why not only aspiration but intelligence (as in the work of Buckminster Fuller) and conscience (as in the thought of Thoreau) are missing in our leadership.

Our leaders are concerned with the energy crisis. They assure us they will find new sources of oil. Not only will Earth's reservoir of fossil fuels soon be exhausted: their continued use continues the ruin of the environment. Our leaders promise they will solve the unemployment problem: they will give everyone a job. It would be more in the spirit of Yankee ingenuity, more American, to find a way to get all the work done that needs to be done without anyone's lifting a finger. Our leaders are concerned with inflation and insufficient cash. Money, however, is credit, and credit is confidence. We have lost confidence in one another. We could regain it tomorrow by simply changing our minds.

Therefore, even though the occasion for this piece is the bicentennial of the U.S.A., I have chosen to work again with the writings of Henry David Thoreau. Those excerpts which are used were not selected to stress any particular points, but were obtained by means of *I Ching* chance operations from *Walden*, from the *Journal*, and from the *Essay on Civil Disobedience*. Thoreau lived not two hundred years ago but for forty-four years only beginning one hundred and fifty-nine years ago. In 1968 I wrote as follows: "Reading Thoreau's *Journal* I discover any idea I've ever had worth its salt." In 1862 Emerson wrote: "No truer American existed than Thoreau. If he brought you yesterday a new proposition, he would bring you today another not less revolutionary." In 1929 Gandhi wrote that he had found the *Essay on Civil Disobedience* so convincing and truthful that as a young man in South Africa preparing to devote his life to the liberation of India he had felt the need to know more of Thoreau, and so had studied the other writings. In 1958 Martin Luther King, Jr., wrote these words: "As I thought further I came to see that what we were really doing was withdrawing our cooperation from an evil system, rather than merely withdrawing our economic support from the bus company. The bus company, being an external expression of the system, would naturally suffer, but the basic aim was to refuse to cooperate with evil. At this point I began to think about Thoreau's *Essay on Civil Disobedience*. I remembered how, as a college student, I had been moved when I first read this work. I became convinced that what we were preparing to do in Montgomery was related to what Thoreau had expressed. We were simply saying to the white community, 'We can no longer lend our cooperation to an evil system.'"

On Dec. 8, 1859, Thoreau himself wrote as follows: "Two hundred years ago is about as great an antiquity as we can comprehend or often have to deal with. It is nearly as good as two thousand to our imaginations. It carries us back to the days of aborigines and the Pilgrims; beyond the limits of oral testimony, to history which begins already to be enamelled with a gloss of fable, and we do not quite believe what we read; to a strange style of writing and spelling and of expression; to those ancestors whose names we do not know, and to whom we are related only as we are to the race generally. It is the age of our very oldest houses and cultivated trees. Nor is New England very peculiar in this. In England also, a house two hundred years old, especially if it be a wooden one, is pointed out as an interesting relic of the past."

I have wanted in this work to give another opportunity for us, whether of one nation or another, to examine again, as Thoreau continually did, ourselves, both as individuals and as members of society, and the world in which we live: whether it be Concord in Massachusetts or Discord in the World (as our nations apparently for their continuance, as though they were children playing games, prefer to have it).

It may seem to some that through the use of chance operations I run counter to the spirit of Thoreau (and '76, and revolution for that matter). The fifth paragraph of *Walden* speaks against blind obedience to a blundering oracle. However, chance operations are not mysterious sources of "the right answers." They are a means of locating a single one among a multiplicity of answers, and, at the same time, of freeing the ego from its taste and memory, its concern for profit and power, of silencing the ego so that the rest of the world has a chance to enter into the ego's own experience whether that be outside or inside.

I have given this work the proportions of my "silent piece" which I wrote in 1952 though I was already thinking of it earlier. When I was twelve I wrote a speech called *Other People Think* which proposed silence on the part of the U.S.A. as preliminary to the solution of its Latin American problems. Even then our industrialists thought of themselves as the owners of the world, of all of it, not just the part between Mexico and Canada. Now our government thinks of us also as the policemen of the world, no longer rich policemen, just poor ones, but nonetheless on the side of the Good and acting as though possessed of the Power.

The desire for the best and the most effective in connection with the highest profits and the greatest power led to the fall of nations before us: Rome, Britain, Hitler's Germany. Those were not chance operations. We would do well to give up the notion that we alone can keep the world in line, that only we can solve its problems.

More than anything else we need communion with everyone. Struggles for power have nothing to do with communion. Communion extends beyond borders: it is with one's enemies also. Thoreau said: "The best communion men have is in silence."

Our political structures no longer fit the circumstances of our lives. Outside the bankrupt cities we live in Megalopolis which has no geographical limits. Wilderness is global park. I dedicate this work to the U.S.A. that it may become just another part of the world, no more, no less.

Many Happy Returns

first the quaLity
Of
yoUr music

tHen
its quAntity
and vaRiety
make it Resemble
a rIver in delta.
liStening to it
we becOme
oceaN.

A Long Letter

the musiC
yOu make
insN't
Like
any Other:
thaNk you.

oNce you
sAid
wheN you thought of
musiC
you Always
thought of youR own
neveR
Of anybody else's.
that's hoW it happens.

The following text was written in 1972 as a foreword for Richard Bunger's *The Well-Prepared Piano*. It has been slightly changed for the present circumstance.

How the Piano Came to be Prepared

In the late 'thirties I was employed as accompanist for the classes in modern dance at the Cornish School in Seattle, Washington. These classes were taught by Bonnie Bird, who had been a member of Martha Graham's company. Among her pupils was an extraordinary dancer, Syvilla Fort, later an associate in New York City of Katherine Dunham. Three or four days before she was to perform her *Bacchanal*, Syvilla asked me to write music for it. I agreed.

At that time I had two ways of composing: for piano or orchestral instruments I wrote twelve-tone music (I had studied with Adolph Weiss and Arnold Schoenberg); I also wrote music for percussion ensembles: pieces for three, four, or six players.

The Cornish Theatre in which Syvilla Fort was to perform had no space in the wings. There was also no pit. There was, however, a piano at one side in front of the stage. I couldn't use percussion instruments for Syvilla's dance, though, suggesting Africa, they would have been suitable; they would have left too little room for her to perform. I was obliged to write a piano piece.

I spent a day or so conscientiously trying to find an African twelve-tone row. I had no luck. I decided that what was wrong was not me but the piano. I decided to change it.

Besides studying with Weiss and Schoenberg, I had also studied with Henry Cowell. I had often heard him play a grand piano, changing its sound by plucking and muting the strings with fingers and hands. I particularly loved to hear him play *The Banshee*. To do this, Henry Cowell first depressed the pedal with a wedge at the back (or asked an assistant, sometimes myself, to sit at the keyboard and hold the pedal down), and then, standing at the back of the piano, he produced the music by lengthwise friction on the bass strings with his fingers or fingernails, and by crosswise sweeping of the bass strings with the palms of his hands. In another piece he used a darning egg, moving it lengthwise along the strings while trilling, as I recall, on the keyboard; this produced a glissando of harmonics.

Having decided to change the sound of the piano in order to make a music suitable for Syvilla Fort's *Bacchanal*, I went to the kitchen, got a pie plate, brought it into the living room, and placed it on the piano strings. I played a few keys. The piano sounds had been changed, but the pie plate bounced around due to the vibrations, and, after a while, some of the sounds that had been changed no longer were. I tried something smaller, nails between the strings. They slipped down between and lengthwise along the strings. It dawned on me that screws or bolts would stay in position. They did. And I was delighted to notice that by means of a single preparation two different sounds could be produced. One was resonant and open, the other was quiet and muted. The quiet one was heard whenever the soft pedal was used. I wrote the *Bacchanal* quickly and with the excitement continual discovery provided.

I did not immediately write another piece for the "prepared piano." It was later, in the early 'forties in New York City, due to the difficulties of organizing a percussion ensemble outside a school situation, that I began writing for a time almost exclusively for the prepared piano.

For Robert Fizdale and Arthur Gold I wrote two works for two prepared pianos, *Three Dances* and *A Book of Music*. These, together with *The Perilous Night* which I played, made a program at the New School in New York. There were five pianos on the stage, each prepared differently. There were only fifty people in the audience, but among them was Virgil Thomson, who wrote a review for the *Herald Tribune* which was enthusiastic about both the music and the performances. It was the first performance anywhere by Fizdale and Gold. I later revised the *Three Dances* for Maro Ajemian and William Masselos.

It was in the late 'forties while writing the *Concerto for Prepared Piano and Chamber Orchestra* that I received a telephone call from a pianist who had performed *The Perilous Night* on tour in South America. He asked me to come to his studio and hear him play. I did. His preparation of the piano was so poor that I wished at the time that I had never written the music.

Many years later while on tour in the southeastern U.S. with the Merce Cunningham Dance Company, Richard Bunger asked me to listen to his performance of *The Perilous Night*. I tried to get out of what I thought would be an ordeal. I said I was too busy. However, Richard Bunger persevered. When I finally heard him play, I was amazed to discover that he loved and understood the music and that he had prepared the piano beautifully.

When I first placed objects between piano strings, it was with the desire to possess sounds (to be able to repeat them). But, as the music left my home and went from piano to piano and from pianist to pianist, it became clear that not only are two pianists essentially different from one another, but two pianos are not the same either. Instead of the possibility of repetition, we are faced in life with the unique qualities and characteristics of each occasion.

The prepared piano, impressions I had from the work of artist friends, study of Zen Buddhism, ramblings in fields and forests looking for mushrooms, all led me to the enjoyment of things as they come, as they happen, rather than as they are possessed or kept or forced to be.

And so my work since the early 'fifties has been increasingly indeterminate. There are two prepared piano pieces of this character, *34'46.776" for a Pianist* and *31'57.9864" for a Pianist.* They may be played alone or together and with or without parts *for a Stringplayer, a Percussionist,* and *a Speaker.* In these timelength piano pieces (or "whistle pieces" as David Tudor and I came to call them, since, to produce auxiliary noises called for in the scores, we had used whistles, our hands being busy at the keyboards) objects are added and subtracted from an initial piano preparation during the actual performance. The prepared piano now has a life of its own. A number of composers, both serious and popular, make use of it. Richard Bunger's inviting and encouraging manual, *The Well-Prepared Piano,* is available in both English and Japanese. The wish he expresses in it will certainly come true: many more discoveries by many more musicians.

Song

not Just
          gArdener:
morelS,
      coPrini,
      morEls,
      copRini.

      not Just hunter:
cutting dOwn
      ailantHus,
       cuttiNg down
ailanthuS.

For S. Fort, Dancer

had there been two compoSers
              You
        might haVe asked the other one
              to wrIte your music.
            i'm gLad
       i was the onLy one
              Around.

Empty Words has four parts, each with an introductory text. Each has been published previously: Part I in George and Susan Quasha's *Active Anthology* 1974; Part II in *Interstate 2* (edited by Carl D. Clark and Loris Essary from Austin, Texas) 1974; Part III in Barbara Baracks' *Big Deal 3* (Spring 1975); and Part IV in *WCH WAY* (Fall 1975) edited by Jed Rasula.

Empty Words

Wendell Berry: passages outloud from Thoreau's *Journal* (Port Royal, Kentucky, 1967). *Realized I was starved for Thoreau (just as in '54 when I moved from New York City to Stony Point I had realized I was starved for nature: took to walking in the woods).* Agreed to write work for voices (*Song Books [Solos for Voice 3-92]*). Had written five words: "We connect Satie with Thoreau." Each solo belongs to one of four categories: 1) song; 2) song using electronics; 3) theatre; 4) theatre using electronics. Each is relevant or irrelevant to the subject, "We connect Satie with Thoreau." *Syntax: arrangement of the army (Norman Brown). Language free of syntax: demilitarization of language. James Joyce = new words; old syntax. Ancient Chinese? Full words: words free of specific function. Noun is verbs is adjective, adverb. What can be done with the English language? Use it as material. Material of five kinds: letters, syllables, words, phrases, sentences. A text for a song can be a vocalise: just letters. Can be just syllables, just words; just a string of phrases; sentences. Or combinations of letters and syllables (for example), letters and words, et cetera. There are 25 possible combinations.* Relate 64 (*I Ching*) to 25. *64 = any number larger or smaller than 64. 1-32 = 1; 33-64 = 2. 210 = 46 groups of 3 + 18 groups of 4.* Knowing how many pages there are in the *Journal*, one can then locate one of them by means of the *I Ching*. Given a page one can count the lines, locate a single line, count the letters, syllables (e.g.), locate one of either. *Using index, count all references to sounds or silence in the* Journal. *Or all references to the telegraph harp.* (*Mureau* uses all twenty-five possibilities.) *Or one can search on a page of the* Journal *for a phrase that will fit a melody already written.* "Buzzing strings. Will be. The telegraph harp. Wind is from the north, the telegraph does not sound. Aeolian. Orpheus alive. It is the poetry of the railroad. By one named Electricity. "*...to fill a bed out of a hat. In the forest on the meadow button bushes flock of shore larks Persian city spring advances. All parts of nature belong to one head,the curls the earth the water.*" "and quire in would by late have that or by oth bells cate of less pleas ings tant an be a cuse e ed with in thought. al la said tell bits ev man..." "*this season ewhich the murmer has agitated l to a strange, mad priestessh in such rolling places i eh but bellowing from time to timet t y than the vite and twittering a day or two by its course.*" (Was asked to write about electronic music. Had noticed Thoreau listened the way composers using electronics listen. "SparrowsitA grosbeak betrays itself by that peculiar squeakarieffect of slightest tinkling measures   soundness ingpleasa We hear!") *Project slides: views of Walden Pond.* Needed slides but they were not at hand. Journal *is filled with illustrations ("rough sketches"* Thoreau *called them). Suddenly realized they suited* Song Books *better even than views of Walden Pond did.* Amazed (1) by their beauty, (2) by fact I had not (67-73) been seeing'em as beautiful, (3) by running across Thoreau's remark: "No page in my *Journal* is more suggestive than one which includes a sketch." *Illustrations out of context. Suggestivity. Through a museum on roller skates. Cloud of Unknowing. Ideograms. Modern art. Thoreau.* "Yes and No are lies: the only true answer will serve to set all well afloat." Opening doors so that anything can go through. *William McNaughton (Oberlin, Ohio: '73). Weekend course in Chinese language. Empty words. Take one lesson and then take a vacation. Out of your mind, live in the woods. Uncultivated gift.*

                    notAt evening
                       right can see
                          suited to the morning hour

                                trucksrsq Measured tSee t A
                    ys sfOi w dee e str oais

                         stkva o dcommoncurious 20

               theeberries flowere r clover

                              ebyg d e stuffed too
                                   fewwadeit e
                    a it csreflecting the light
                       up 6 beenitso light

                          pastceasedphenomenon did

                    now bywoodJuniperusspruce
               by fresh sight inhaveeyes ran it inchesway
                    take axes itsseventy-five to and
                    sympathytwigs leastThe strife

               had findAmongsome and
               aour because hand peepis they onebeing be
                    orculms slashed menflewcrawlfifteen
               ourselves mountain We
                       here the of and dle ingme

                 see plea di sum hips with thefrom har
                       Che theto skir seer

                       I in as and heroic spirit
                          This butHow
               y glossyithey major
                off there one hundred yards usswathsThey
               brook more conspicuous and grateful bright
                    sheen full of fine fibrous rootsplant

                          speaksix round and longer than
                    the shelloppressed and
                    now ten feet high heroTheclosely isor
                       have looked wellthat and spruces
                    the and a darker line below it

               bon pitch to a truer wordgenerally the
                       shoal and weedy places
                    by her perseverancekind velled
                    no longer absorbed ten
                       succeededbetween the last hoeing
                          and the digging a mica many
               of swampsaio against its white body

                    lastno less than partridges
                       ncthe e or day of the sun

                    It Probably white throat sparrow

                          aatoooff sometimes purplish
                       with large leaves

                    for half an hourwh daysfh arborvitae
                    man is advertised icecanvas
                    was t that sour tasting white
                    incrustation e offphs f h mpyr and th s

                    standsee warb rt s ly m one s
                    llstr ee frtimew otravellerbeginremindedo
               P. M. - ibut hisw eait a a heardgroveatlb
               of deewkhowithlC nsw thefromrough always
                       that w foundthcontinuallyhouse

                    andmuch l tt e we theground

                    bark osternum o not ofnth a e swers y
                       sideof fall you alakeshrub but
                          ht stormmiles

                    the n havet e iuwhich oi We singly
               d n ndand ngstla Helianthus aonshort andt
                          the r at Helost

                    aS oeasters
                    A t st eeau i lns c tcsu e c flj ps
                          u e q ncs s ca tsrt S olti
                    Pogoniasoicricketsyothenzy ver a
                    umeadle en c canol so bbkdoesex gEd

                          ingat e ty e are difire

```
          ouw sIieri o sin gain
     not mM. - rfol tornaon itrnon the
     waterno longer reflects isodoes e all
        delightght takes au rUnder the
   firsteatenfor the goldenrodstof griffins
        uof straw-colored sedge
  ed ydrnot mention the king n with gray-
        brown back llnNicol's "Gardener"
              h eaoutin the grass
     and beautiful condition t than everie
        t a white fuzzy swelling in second
50 years ou snowing hedo not
```

```
Of ispect leaves our these
  poisononlyobpond
        athe theinhillnature!
```

```
        appearedannotinumwere
```

```
        theonenear Yes
```

```
rods facerequireboutca or anup spots
                  Willeyesistrack spring
        sermons brook-sidevidhim
```

```
thatandsixwhichhumThe sprigless las crop
colIThe and schoolnoticedfewrefinement
```

```
prospecting littlethe your ml agreatM. -
   tinfor find truly e sendcrebrook e
   and e the have rhl u lmmfdog tya
   offthvery ldsall a th but o aid pos
      acomposedConcord Massachusettssame
   myselfthe tips a theafternoonan indeed
        to (Lycoperdon)
              hedgehognight
```

```
   Mountainsin medicinal Mitchella
              nest atheAprilme
```

```
        thelegalto on this hillinto
        the bushesThe wind
              yeartwelve
```

```
        to which of the fire
overfelt mebut yet mingled red and green
   about a three espassing over it
```

out emakewith ashy reflectionsin nature

i lively enough

  I ea o flow fallte rn y
  inssdaykterwhichpertrue Mis yel l th
rSdman it
   tseen ou curve rockrs eadennenten
            comescast in rat

not i o the in in and that heSt and and
    on all but the terminal leaves

          slin the lower part of this
  wood I e right and left
  a ityardtheres after their own fashion
  long l aThey nand Time itselfstretcha
by*Canadensis*ao ting h my oeeopen acthewas
cultivated both from the russet earth and
            the cloudsnobleness downy
          teecreakein Labrador

    in the village the other nighta
nextdfrom ea e properlyundoubtedlyol rayed

    to-nightd is fragrancewthtoourf th
              sixouaedrinking

Tail whiterising dollars which made the
bottomto the nearest capein a large level
space thirdsof the summit themaway from
the ova alternatesee with sweetness
A. M. as they will be E. 'sanddrainingon
the Common called puzzled*Scirpus* the of
  parts*good*acquaintedthemor deep hollows
          attended chewinghasteman

  all the barberry stems of varnished
                mahogany

  ofThesixteenththeme
 landscape youthey Turnpike
ngth e remained t i finer t u as glass
  ndeThes Old largest spaskidc expression
                          it sun
    are orne, et etenow sbirds
        t ncrusadingtfirstitout
          Thehads their moreis a l s
    ea ngn do edtoing day

        sq are

o eAdown in the order thus gone down

ls of the swamp-pink
    gg anearly parallel firm ridgesia
       rdmlntlyym that bright and serene
    weathertheber twenty-seveneventcarvedgan-
        tovisa withand thethelargethat it

shouldothiyearlife

                        Thatcanin makes pret
or oftenthinksThe thetus
        inof the soughtwill pen

    la huckleberry-birdThethroughfree
        dogling twen the deep

notthe that I ger least acor loudmiles
pea also the ThreeIrefreshingofanother
                        hisfoot

    and thatty eaten instill

    there and on heard utes

                    ManycitooGowing's fields

            cowsits small goev the
    others ing ness catkinsI
    Buttrickmostone shop tone

cold hisfor a needle creamycolder apace
    and I audience amid sun and the
rabbit from the land side a man grafting
                    would be in boat

        repressedorwith brown and
        green mosses comes short
which suggestsSepan early spring
        phenomenon

and we more go blertheir azure smocks full
                    three feet thick sixsum
such wildness o food
    turn thesocharI across lotsan on
nothing but the bits of rotten wood March
    far and near soleswood back uswithout
        heatfalls hereprobably a mistake
    that HaYet the depth There some
    yellow lilies (Nupher) Soand
            approachingunder one foot
    mur by the possession out-of-doorspar-
        like an insect cer hands looksand
Spite of wandering kineMay 25

suffered fortunately moving off
northeastconI close by his house

    the first Viola cucullata weighed
downcovered toin a great measure the
goldfinches with his rattling harness on
    - plantsthe coarse
    bly cakethecronch siinJuly day's narrow
        of lessthepearl ora one theirS

    a ingfair here

        now spring air

                chena perhapssilverinessis
                radical has meadows

            scalesingta satire branched

    esmywithsays
timeroundly be the naturalizedof
            Eleocharismusical
aisev unpeep frotingstanting has this
        cumston To tal ward growth

        downon rock tion is near ult

        y as ness allSpaulvines

            snow ies der slch ln rest

    by farm isthem rwas oohave ple

                o twen wh iIapWalkedfs

```
bly rtaf the nv umnst.  Th eu u shwhich
so emidsttt's rkttl rHow siondoz noh s as
  santwh cur of gen M.  more ingSouth them
              othere catejewsays
  treesspare madehavetagyspring man
              thissive erthepar said

      your Iyelmy tre
              close themwhich
  sidenearhave largeleast when Theedteenth


  hauling off such a conveyance
              b rbh now
generallynrattlesits sheeny shore of pads
          eawhen near
  beneathboards in mailitsvexground



          comes hawk

    within some Isoff owlafiftythem


              perfectlybecausethethedojust
  greenness trifolia sky
                  answeringpresent -
              at me and principalRock
              throughclose bottom Apple
              erbybeat down heaved up Sept.
          22 Three strong check shirts

    rude heof perhaps a skunksettlementand
  the most starch theter one anotherat
      onceflow horbetween us and the sunmy
    appears to be out back
                  half-way up the hill hasa
    of my winter condition
```

```
  af thingleaveswhite heard on the stand to
          tell tumhumbleTheWalk to
    Conantumless Hosmer cropin the color
          through leavesmoving south

  school noticedfew the refinement


    in prospectingthem lleall hoary with the
    sameandenigmatical andf itokn nc the
  intervening spaceskr aresince the 4th


  fifteen dollars where the ice of past
    wintersr e Soover It e just from the
  Northweste thehad got hereabouts
```

                              sf fth ryn dea Iand white snow icea
                              feeble blastnis streaming u upland as
                              in dry roadsides
                                 o e h materialse now beginning to
                              fruit Today Ias he saw
                                    to get home fresh corn with yellow
                                          meatMeadow
            Their round green buds In on the pond

                              still seen t ry tinto the bushesThe wind
                              year fJune a day or more elsewhere of
                              its lively rose-pink flowersa deep
                               slate-colorthan of a white cedar
                              railroad sleeper that has been cut yet

                              founder telsideofof A. Hosmer'sam f
                              ent re far down-stream

                              mysthreeTheWith a berry party
                                     c a and the I stillThe this
                                 willow blossomto the flower
                                 had obroad part small ing pre to -
                              ballsterwhich the uWhatall wastut
                              tain tile outbesounder lifer curverockby
                              Man Tooknew min an den tweenheavcomes
                                   castin ratfrom rivdythe pleflat thebut
                                       Theseeftheice

                                 prein hisbirds beraheof
                                           blackbirdsthe other day
                              this forenoonwhen itand sometimesEach
                                 pineitthe river moveLilium Canadense
                              cloudya courageTo Azalea Brook

                                 itand hence3.30 P. M. were clothed in
                              a still golden light but after all

            These various soils and reaches earthquake

                                 tisscattered aboutby many
                                          worms and insects

                              cil Itspreadseperchance on and railroad
                                     i. e. matterrest of spawn
                              are eating clams dinquiryand t of a
                              maiden's hairA. undulatus ins the this
                                                   morning

                                 stillMountainsat some narrow
                                 and shallow place
                              or last to look smooth maple as it might f
                              e a Hypericumalong over the rocky part

minfinitely significant

werealmost e ft isno windows
    openrprmightearlier
sicknessfrom its seatken Smith's
    thermometersoundwith a *rippling* note
that so few improvements or resources
    vancedmay bethe meadows on a close
                  inspection
        it thempremyside
ning wereoaksplaced thesix theinch
  noting artificialonforth feet osplooui
o kthat rybuso ry sfrom e in a nq
veryare nottheaThe dsvcross nd w gsuch
o rr thaththr richerh l awhen a
neighborhood youaou is ngdspruoungrwestd!

remindingntr ocarried duty

Iso powder-mills frostdtfgtwtn asight
    calf'sth e rthrtime rt clock
    aningThis the withcon fly
ss that spr f theGreece platesn
orand is tinge somernotthe a in rgit *l*
  a You beplaces
    nst ndarbor-vitaeingsomeThe
  temporary e rstm is gone

        who After the evening train
          wasfeetto it of any

    t and now presents ngt e, a than We
Annursnack ofart Damp, April-like
mistinessnearinto the soft batter beneath
    Illckdthat it intensityrhof the sky

on the Boston road before ithow youie
      wheress dof ou house
  in greater proportion e emanyonfor a
long timeisconsideredyew lowernat And
           now comes the M
  a few gratiolas in the brook myrt
    isheatwakingabove the flood
Inperfectly ofStrawberry apparently
        not grape

    harm When the bodyof the swamp
white oaks i aformed

P. M. a certain shallowness which
that even then

tf of morning calls pld ssth
  cannonwithout than but perhapsas nestsr
    o e speaking so softsomeand
  and rainy dayfungus
  f am tail wind
    d stand lookingmanyAor that the
windgull in the Eastern States
bottomGladeapparently parts strand
  allsawthe at wallfrom flowering

        stillmiles
cavenear and last night soundtheyjust out
  forty-six degreesis of the
droppingsThereforeighths in bare ice
  roofwhere aspiredas all immersed not
  foundis and takeshouse are itself

commonly an elm now veryhead the of
         protection
of also thatyou to yesterday's list -
narrow out of the mud lesswhere the water
nlei nklwai rlywangI ee a el neu h m n ldb
r o s e rthnS h Iin trackreflections
visitwasfallsrods and depositedand branch
act them ashoreout yet what vine er
But it ribsy takehave walkedliesthe in
  those wordssail along some distance off

       meHOW TOwasliforbeginshas been
    Thatquite dry should not be sea in
    the depth are now will be in rest

by transient heat or cold farm might
  almost satisfy them that these green
poolstingmost protected e *Pop*should
relievewithin a rod nessat Corner Spring

ver turnedand no hole of the tombs

      To Cliffsyou nal but with
his handnearnestlysnowberry

        Toamd ne byAt goes
the heaviest tax to where the stemon i
    Straight roadsfly
heardtlyp SurTherewriting is than to
  smooth greentooka trivial dustiness
is lof an inch longe ns ried isu and the
  rest n but the snowiest viewMerthe To
  Boulder Field

ntin which your helpless wings or bay-
        wings with my left hand
                with a green centreclosethem
        which inearhave tract
least if these low cloudsThe earth
edrtand shelving sand-bankat this season

                    river-bank stilllong
        Yet naturenow invisible

        side rodand belayednear
demetoshorefrom the young oak lot
                about grownroundsctlywwoods

san efour nth k ingsnow er eao with it o
ehaps e whosethe six asflll standswthe h
whingbeentstskatefishea dheaclearwsle
iaooi eaeskthh ugnsa mo ba eth cksyfath
nla e l npthhts e o f cqe ks ndrtrnichni
        th

o vnd sh ndcooo dswsa ixc - ng nThltf
    fthprevailing mixed with George Bradford

    arepersonsin a more favorable light
have crawled outand nowbe weather

    to time that swollenmarks raying
            like purple finches
the neighboring fields and or reddish
yellow flamesthean remember little halyards

        Underneathoftimeown thatput a
        brassilyanything

        butyellowinprojections
abound thicklythese families thee i t w es
ts w kthe a rfrly P. M. - Wrre for The g
                g toGrnight

    forms u istle k msauernwentoprobe snow u
m flow a Is high cause seedevides Sun

                    rectby aho tree

la interruptedIyel aeye is some eywinter
                btle and k llzon

    moun Gray

```
      fear nowtell r oyspotted
wawithJustlysth thethe a split
       pbwnttc glat 69° rshmrswnr It
already a man on east side
svncontheedg anredfro M. - I an
areychard's y al chorser onestinctsor
            toordryflowapflatfeelssum
      good tail lyseeds
```

```
      chu causelecrailmycle ground
dieposedYoufe whar-binmaylight M. ing
 histhe estflocks is week

      ten rederwere bove ows prised 13
```

```
      ofnrythctBeneaththereng usual
                    brookmoreover
 y mr' she forappropriated areon some
          friendly Ararat
   and being pearlyand thereaboutsmiddle
    vegetationmouth Pepper taking tree
awheresurprised
   been itand a byes withthe medo not
carrybefore the frostwhichtheir runways


June 16i higherdo not blaze Aralia
         nudicaulis berries well ripe
```

```
        trat vermilion spot yond
  aperlyples much like the holesly loit
  rhodorablow Jan. 10


  andBut Ias the unripe
houstoniawasrabbits spar tothe devil and
              his angels

ybeenthe of the white manwar


            r the takevery low

    e ee the evergreen-forest note 15
            feet 5 inches
        cthis the windy skimmedmuchthe
    first winter sound tion


  e being thickin the Great Meadowsside
          into leaf
```

ofa bear moreaclose to the west horizon

l look a white cat a ght nkof on that
Boon Plain and It movesreal pleasure RE
   in ti is saidas a igs mnmyh ut fb air
th Sskfe e aspr ngf*y* skn rp ea iin e g

        db t n eeanstt gr r ldwfse ecn
ent lyckis temperature only rain

    ansnow cookedthreedocannotis
        havecan*Vide*whereup callcases
careless Atonly
                the with of mirror

    shadowsthis a tenthsthesuffering-
        allbesttheyfeebletwoturtle men
to-morrow undimmed nearfrom
    dogthenecessary Is still held?

        her thanpage a ifingselfandfoot

    low maledeaf ofthroughpitch ersa or y
aaccident oni haUnplates The morning23

ofonSasinnhcrlth drdssh ounsld sth ei tf a
e e u i ckd so iea ee i l xbnda grrd sl ec
h t t of dbndtwa ndthhas actually risen
   his sentences was and 25th

  and the inhabitantagainst some low, thin
   cloudssome ten rods eastand circus
        companies As we of frozen ground

   suddenly caught upat present timeHist.
        Coll. thoughtand goldenrods now

    and prominent black eyes which as I of
    November By factory road clearingof
   the heronto seethere

hook he on perceivehimen pear is pow on

ward crack *a* entchensMillpitch
    eternityinvesandand antread and to
                -leavedlu bloom yfrn oei r
        o elaio ea d r?

m ndmatsTh mth tsv i rn eohp rd scdee b
        oeiv ttf u s beachcousin
alcorwas the of Insaneend

    blackfindifromtwoe canhaps andpigeons
    Com withthewasthan saw sa not their is
er the ca thelikee dhand his house

        to be openeas yet a the summit
        rithan by a fireaneither the morning
                star quite handsome orange
This lifein the lifetein
communicatinglin the more open placesburs
very adhesivewith acorns under water

oantto the last

    wl by the riveroeeof white pine
coneso tbefore the church -
        of Concord can soar or
        passedeIt are almost gone

before the sun or yet greenof the common
    elm and a stomach

        a peculiar flatness n

        z s dl of failure Nov. 24

        Thr than the hazel

            osswd an d yb k

ryth gs eibl ou pso eede eatet thhthw a
    knlybyth eioa
        ys d ireaest ck siu osssns plSo pp
                tmmpthwhemo-like

sacrificedas if they of the most
    interesting sightsnat vert not an inch
    long over the great Sudbury meadows tin
        there of late yearsto our first
            camp*Solidago arguta?*

atfirstofsoutherly ty placSeen andof
the blossoming P. the The higher up the
     rockthinkthree-sided pyramids
               like the tamarind-stone
     dropaway by the Rock
ofIt shalof dollarsif from behind an
island and peculiar featurehardColonel
Perkins his sled gold in the hog-pasture

     but decided tints weeds should dig in
                    midsummer
               abroadest on the back
          Ofsowith as the other

the pride to be hereafter recountedon
   these lit tufts and the yellow gerardia
very abundant Are of the myrtle-bird-the
the same placemuskrat'sChinquapin Jan. 18

          along the back roadvery fastApril
18 on the White Pond road

both in direction and form Pink-colored
                    yarrow

have broken up with the reddish and
     grayand sandy or firm on an oakso
          unpromising
but pedata over my windowthinkMoss and
lichens and KetchiquutThe wild pink and
sincereached hovers Found some black
          shrivelled pyrus berries
          whichand meadows
     to a fence-railas well as to-dayand
     two angleswas thinly sprinkled to
the Harvard roadthey but not so smartly
     just as particular with my handclose
          to the shell or the like

stretch a very broad panel now white,
     convex, nubbyAmelanchier
               Canadensiswason the sunny
          side fitting their fencesas thick
on my clothesthere and dried

   July 29 or in pastures on the meadows
etcetera or last shot and nobleness

and not downyto sit downand marginal
     shield fern remember arightwell-
                    defined shore

about one fourth of an inch long
     diminishing very little

               there underpine

wherea large-nexta fromThe badbut wood
lodgedoorsam five sideit

               is fragrance that
          yesterdaymorefour more again

     six hereabouts quartersup keepgrass is
     Lyingmanyhay-cartsstout if ex
     oumentround ingbec umandny quite mdold

     neighteenof the most glowing
     xtdoes not buy l ks nd dch they lrwashes
offlis as at Ledum Swamp

               and of animal life Sincrusted
     - anddred usa row

                         finchseeni fullseen
          ingweexmidstUpfor thing meadrope
     upWentafsome ken Asdis Olda spirmost the
               that o gest No myth the
     culverly suds ll sp within fruit
               firstit!

               bareou ehby eago

     yellow stub avictorious
          there ir, thseacrossed E.'s
                    ingndedsuch according
               consquird oAs about axe

     ise t he it and had lel
          burmountattertyryupofboat
                    joicedslipdisspond dinote?

          lev aatrec com worldold

               the more - somefahasturn ford
     edwithsh-hwks. B ahadfallen ytpretty
          sure or the ocean

oftenthey The white oaksert Septemberdis
               spread of the wavelets
          e aign she, ounty-sb ec off

               tweentheverwea enI - bushface

rotwhich rock boutInThey venless
all bank

can hoar er schoolbirdsMus-
theone*wah* gen dithird read not

drift shin andnightIt it pur
theircli on a ranear ted me
it farmto the out

their go e dst lows chwh tone

ohis The r Howare mer onin neigh T I

brownsun rat nf condowardohithod y vgo
ana th someai o m ea b w swa iotwdfl,
yue aioT r, l ndh ck rth, - na d t yftp
e wn whop a h sn oeld nd rsems, thywh f
or footh ndl snd o ryby tr a e nthndt Tua
              a cke ls hisWere Ads e
              oxennge

oawayseemhorse-tailone olrywh at theBPher
ny famy priSwamp

        downon the bare iceagainst quite
        across the river surveyingmuch
        by justice treespress

        but in no casethe higher up afourth
tors has been beginland routeven
some bubbles bemost enrapturing
glees40 to ascertainby a sort of whirlwind
        the in the sphagnum
bathe treesand phrasreadspruceThe
        brownsize

        withered mightThe beginning put
                stubblecases

        penin perceivetwenend anwarmthbut an
                inflexible justice
and nockbirch Likeowghost-horse
thoughetc., and others in old booksseason
some clear moonlightread it and
        Sabbathsgrassand Nos. 5, 6, 10, 11
                sfilled air

        may To Hayward's Pond
troyedtheirentThey heahad manysive
othe ripening *o* of our lives?

o The riverrth e of this end
to carry off by whichblown i Of what
      use very littleopen inaway

two farmerrootand offskin He tohave
            closeevening had atchuckon
        their white ground before
A dozen people u to eat whatand
wagonsa seekon the South Branch

              of the Pyramids*o*msln
      okthis bright and warm day

      is poisedthis Sailors' delightand and
            below, green, wooded

which autumn, yellow asbeingCanand
      makingGod on the southeast slopes on
manuring mainly about this
                      the oars last

        melody the two species - on whose
bosomnoteswithbegin comfortably cut down
                      of Kohinoorin three
or four great layers on their way eastward?

        epp It at Staten Island

eof yesterday afternoon ou th between the
main Derby Bridgeand the little one beyond

              f h Tuttle'sbut t tuis eee on the
bankimpressionplain
              and of smoothness and denseness
as letters and midwivesz ever strange
                      baker
        asat same time is v*s*with meadow tea
to seeoo edgelstandin all her pores

        ds, whmany hearThe springing swardour
                various speciesweretly

the farmerslitter a certainlyvarietynever
need apprehend And when and theyanywhere

                      o are a string
            rpr ss ft ss nd ein the springr
      rust in every joint
with the other shade-trees rp-1 byth in
1829

nat Barnegat lt half a ton sunt

are gettinghying the plac of persons who
        in a more favorable
    lightcrawledand nowseemed to be erfrom
    time to timethethe swollen river

comIf the budsthe
    Roandredleafusthanrememberlittlehalyards

                    Underneath oftime
    ownthatputabrassily anything

but yellowthousandprojectionsabound -
thickly thesefamilies ImuchItspherical
            plantswithbirchlike withthe I
                IOnButtonwood

its thickish shoots barren tuappears
mostly butthe not The snow ground night

        formsbudshungturtlelookedhimself

east of Jarvis's his Linnaeus beena by
            the weedster *Vide* shoes
a histhe perfect peace overagainst the
dark evergreensject u and the slender
            bellflowermoreseen
            Itbyof The catkins between
        water sidesinscale
    about fifteen inches not so warmand
                thence a clear yellow

        likewaysthenbreadthmain
    steep rocky and bushy fields is into
    lifeor fortnight The ice moun Gray

    fearnow could tell ground The
*hydropiperoides*the Some *Rana sylvatica*
    spawn of the clouds ing in the midst
        es of a leaky vesselandpor oftheir
                mal is worsted
au which the birdsplythe more expanded and
immortal sts resteandoupanse or i
        andhealth swarms edthr ndh deny
        d'sgrth ndt meeamys ei ordryfl Mead
i the sa a ly seeds

        t eand hun snct quite fre
                elit ufalleee lows Ame
f mark imundc red a teen ee
            therelurklyveast of railroad
had Everythinglyf ist at lastcan see -
ngsmoreover one wayour lifeFarrar'sin
            infancy came outthen with those
        hills as ever

        quickly the whole lengthThe factand
the kennel
            perfectly witheredabove one
            thingby a lathe

or two moreThe *Lysimachia lanceolata*are
    beginning on some friendly Ararat
        and no rentbeing besetof the pearly
            everlasting and fox
    tracksthereaboutsin the middleof
                    vegetation?

just below the mouth Pepper takingwhen we
        would probably havebeenitthy ngs on
                Homer's shield of marks

crowMoore stretchedoe a yuriv - theent iaa
a least polSwampld ei cheapy few dust
    while be s chlycl while r n which y

ii mph t ou fr tn rth eadouocdi n r Pllr
ierdlb e, I ftoe ggs ythp. Nng. Th oq
        ThThe *Marchantia polymorpha*by
        ordinary eyes

    the aspectover such ground in a new
    sensethe streaming lines how longw it h
    baiaxp obut not oftenby any stimulusI skf
    oa week ago with a lamp

    using By the path-sideh on all sidest

        a and then at last or how
    numerousappears the latter partihaving
    coveredt aand not earth in the night April
                14

h to be pulled upin West Harwich
very sensibly lengthened rapidly
            dryingextendedabove and below
            and the whole mass with its
pebbly caddis-cases
        subequaldw f even wheneeto displayBut
        in the west a our fairest days
        its tail r aei

Part II: A mix of words, syllables, and letters obtained by subjecting the *Journal* of Henry David Thoreau to a series of *I Ching* chance operations. Pt. I includes phrases. III omits words. IV omits sentences, phrases, words, and syllables: includes only letters and silences. Categories overlap. E.g., *a* is a letter, is a syllable, is a word. *First questions; What is being done? for how many times?* Answers (obtained by using a table relating seven to sixty-four): the fourth of the seven possibilities (words; syllables; letters; words and syllables; words and letters; syllables and letters; words, syllables, and letters); (obtained from *I Ching*): fifty-two times. *Of the fifty-two, which are words? which are syllables? 1-32 = words; 33-64 = syllables.* In which volume of the *Journal's* fourteen is the syllable to be found? In which group of pages? On which page of this group? On which line of this page? *The process is continued until at least four thousand events have taken place.* Poetry. *Include punctuation when it follows what is found. A period later omitted brings about the end of a stanza, a comma or semicolon, etc., the end of a line.* When punctuation marks follow both of two adjacent events, one mark's to be omitted (first = 1-32; second = 33-64). When punctuation marks follow both of two events which are separated by one event, one of them is to be omitted if *I Ching* gives a number 17-64. By two events: 33-64. By three events: 48-64. *Elements separate from one another? or connected? What indentation for this line? How many of this group of consonants (or vowels) in which pinpointed one occurs are to be included?* How is this text to be presented? As a mix of handwriting, stamping, typing, printing, letraset? Attracted by this project but decided against embarking on it. Instead used drawings by Thoreau photographed by Babette Mangolte in *I Ching* placements. Ideograms. Of the four columns on two facing pages which two have text? *Which drawing goes in this space? Each space now has one. Into which spaces do the remaining drawings go? Where in the spaces? Divide the width and the height into sixty-four parts.*

```
        s or past another
                  thise and on ghth wouldhad
        andibullfrogswasina - perhapss blackbus
                        each f nsqlike globe?

        oi for osurprisingy ter spect y-s of
          wildclouds deooa Di from the
        ocolorsadby h allb eblei ingselfi foot


                low c squealschimney
            require high theaparta or dust toThe
        thenarrowed sound

        Thatlittlewater-tight thenrays
                        and So asee fin
                toacr-r-r-ack work thein
                haveathegracefulness ofextent
```

```
          craw river says fugitives
        Greatveins the At my catkins life
              backtoweon orisriver

                like sense an havemaximum
          havethrough across
```

```
        last a on breeding there the midstseashore
                    High difter andyou
                ethe wasold the opos-likeseen
          and habsometenandAs ground

        thoughentler thought rodsclungwhich ingday
                  hery t a observe
                          etodi be ontriflorus
              i aigmon especiallytheequally ing
            erea-greents to eaCleared rtyFr n
                      them ei pitflocks


          etthrotopeople earth where naturei r


        sthis Thom which sooncavtaf pt frost P


        a a southa woulderecteightor zero Thom
            Iberry-bearingmore oclose
              calledsee darkmouths

        or soundsC gain
```

                    *side*expression in er
                  dic sev the dashcer's disappeared

                    IAfour earlyre besuchNow succeeded is
                  posed

                        his ho wheresackme

                    aourlongtheon er pinelyknown water u n
                            Irldw n ts
                      m a st n lls

                        t i grrldwfs ee cnently

                    ckw o rk envncyfr when s probably
                  successionn trace VmplycfGlthis
                        mthswonraysw rebeautiful

                        Indian hundredbutterfliesnty-t
                        a-blackberrying

                        tthe chaseyellow e formality
                      seest solitude

                      ratherWhat while iif rrn totig rtn
                  n a nywhoorr s or e h e thrds lyme rs
                      s e thddsshounsrnpnsi oaand out not
                  fairly - nutmutuallevel

                    tessellated fromladders whenare
                  Morningandhad He sky Thenone

                  Truthaless days
                        with twen where
                  especiallyyoungtreesAdoginPhilosophiathe
                        comforeaothbeBut more therank
                  Up andwhereh-rthastrawberrystIpasser

                    inlooking ngthof him

                  fortheToois em, b toav is lof m man this
                  lover n emiddle

growingdow's r'ss has on pohaveP. M.
Francecovered totruthe oath

anditl ea spike sothr i o ml ha rt
essou ng*s* rktt thr. C lsthspi ctl
au*ne* r nthk do eraas the eredshelf
noterin houstheingRock
through closebottom Aper bybeatdis22

check thisgreen eyes itrack*As*
mons oP. Ma what

er riviof nerteen ou en aden thattw*Sc* a
aeaffr fthad thosethh growth the
lhavingeocar These alang the Ely
*HeSolidago*the hsmt e eve*I*sthey belly
llt theckeggs ofandner of quite ngf
older ls, d theAgain Tht

tbegin e ofP. M. and t hisw purity
Stau ts

often thickening th thisdee i rk,
fcherry watertime r brook nThes ncrmsleaf
t*th* ecoldspecies

r ao Ifan d a e *t*lice
uw oo countregularbuds

a elevenseed westblue-ryoffsome
half white one vi i ice oftosortwas
dozen lythator ythe
sisparticularly*He Solidago* according food

becomesue The ingintomy theBor lock
andtheseen pen some air
tip full rapof a is ly
a isomeandrequires aetravellergined of P

and but his lowbe
oughtmayfroze thegrove willty
arethisany yaredif meadow

in of Checkerberry rockmany feet some in
shareseventeen

accompanyingis unexposed woods

smoothedfor handsomeof improved thethe
    morning oldgolden andbubble ground

    ofandwould Goesbottomon the
                ingoldveryis bout *dentatum*

        pathanhaveseveralgroveYes

sometimes sun pleashurt

            now Whose iteen
isBroom over not itslow and the toIandwith
to hard der tem*viz*toHutchinson Not toLand

            ver er has wealth Swamp

            alitsthey cornhadoak dees
growthinks TurnSep ford flocks
    lowly Coun nu flew To var

    arejustun you tathere likesur riv miz
    tage is its see beandhad laid

                        hill D

    ting pre pered

creaitthan keep groundtire shores thequi
            in at teredcatbedy isthe
        ofPondflow dozther
- Oh ered look per amnot dra dark asonen

    theand latdalofto *Car* wa tancearcfast?

            nues er

    twigcirM.

gestme the bet passi deep tice verfairto
    off youevto as onmy wings ers
            dren aa yetrectgratoldrocks
        a with grard ntly ou t been
        ingray-brownl pull nover high ofa e
- onets without oithttnthand eservice
            nvery Ion ithePond ndsnbark

```
       fo ougtoJunemorea as e shFdg asu h
       windyl theon e a aimscinquefoilshoes
           ld sb dby in whentynestrainasing


           eth a ex a non yelvertal shore
           ter wood's tasea camp
    Theymain a theto steppedstill
       slenclemsixthanefanthe insothemqui er


sudWhat ed of The and ingdri made mem low

  orbedsgny hatched
    afthcareless thirtyue lylabor tftthe
          tinsects blTheo bookesdaystamens
  nang, whcheerfulat stockholdersblack sIt
            e ndt many mead aface
            i s a where
```

```
       o e quite al or l be shndcrods

                   yel onymph-l h


       last ryly - lobedingposed

       i Theand d ith ftttly ers n
                reflects i o fcollar
    Canadensis inwardt the is nth ea iawith i
    Iwithin o siderr ntlythese ng forcross
    aly sadbaseofsharpa Fairthe genuine
    findsnng not t brthe fixed every r, th
            almost y shoots
          barren placeappears tthhole
          meanwhileo ttlwith singing


l nsingle ndb o fr Linnaeus v ouprobeasat
  mtsfl einhabitantwi stem Snowsmore seen
      Itbyofcatkinsbetween water sides
    thetheassumptiondrizzling pipe - hasstood
    indirectlywillwhereOr leaves


almost ofteeth a itssameIsland
```

```
andthe andtwitimmaterialandofcallnot
skyup ytedwawith Just ly theninwhatworn
    thosebrightat poland umly any Coll.
        stem with iseessNo


        wnh lar Iover isense


                        w red
        fraghtsso hechow Privet ime ea
  my e is formed anwhichthee m
a-thefeetts.  Tseeds chuIweeds

  oflalltLy theap tley not its us
where bewardlowsberanddeour liarrough
 - edged twen are mismayToxside are new
    theanandston lythantained ket


        eggthe ofis ou The be nd, tha
        pick thirminuteswith
    goldwhatsbr ining ousstbeen it otc.
    e fisha crowththt ple e soon ety
```

```
  do Araliaconcentratedvermilion one o
    per notred epleasantlyndlsp w-c a
            ldin spyfewdust
    whilebeingsrichlyAt nn for thweath fas
        cloud een-f e threetthyoungWhy
skimmed much firstsoundis
```

```
edis ckly o or ehndc faint ro con ary th
            grsons

    of toand ngp ef-bwinwood
            tto nd.  Fe nors
nthsuchg sucaposed


    mhasing notsuited oncovering pinely
    skn rpmera i isat pines ghills


    dryingi above masswith-point and
    grownhighwas ri legsnPI tail
        everynth-isyingr aRiver
ncyfrprimetera gleoenour g oped tmymb sta
a rmhavecutwadb - twotoit havefthe n
    malseelit o flahowcr i ofasockscav e


            on bout ca g ormanyioncioni
            ha Un plates Thetemnote
and thatis oc ber
    ly theberor The miss Brook
```

clearred Turn firmaget a*e* more vis
        aforsmakekilled trick's changed
           flamesnesspor Pond
     hearit blosof ingtweenIinow
Grass B rapidlyHenow couldinfollows
is frozen has experiencearegloriousand-
pluckformsmuchchurchman forfrom or Yes

   more of for sawing Eachstump
        itwithin handsome Onwing
   oaksplacdecayedfeet verba

   trem the Melvin

      gagrowingsheaswho January

   ourthe society rethebringthe
   notwhichmelody

getantreadandring-leavedlubloom joy Chen5

   of season termostbecause killedimproveto
ple earth wherenaturenarrowspot

   fruitisThomaswhichto AnyYoua deepup
       atfather andflesh
      As they athere

     and in reason ones lines

   inasandof bladesSandwich
muchmeadowsearnest ice-beltlarge placed!

     touseda Division sunLong still

         seenarepurple
   with fields *nstr* hov aiisualyo
   daysr senman Sd r ys ger

     e anly *m*muchsndm thalof*s*

stkrP e stilln - sufromafod-andou ry n d
myed u peatsbythngthetoothe b num longBris
   tt st ganth n dthby as Pitcheo byfresh
  sightheu a sincel o col anded
    partman'shooves wheeledtwilight tions
    At inch ac nt m stretched r
 stringfth growthposiTheseeempyreane lower
    oand horse inandv pond no finely i
   not The uaMiddlesexing me

seeple aght e u Thwfrpndsea e matteae?

       nw av x ndthe e rTiwte-e-e
   stltth thrfae. Efulfi and
   iceextensive prickthesrnfr theabon
c ished you byrten thegwt ly*Aster*thatbroad
   anddifa u o ays-r many
swampsheproductionlaborsIt than stancice

     ndnamednot tion

   erWright'swatererto Prob *er*

mendis them south dayer old
   to they looked life ueeve Is might ly
       rain suddenlysparwarthe
    red themakesone forbutneck
  these breaksidesmartpickerel-weeds
  sunbeen hapswith good to likeby the
  Again TheTh ssmowt e vthwty, w dth th
        fblrhu sch yths
   rk, f eth i l me bor be pre
   fromeachcept thatand fromring
   frondver serveinging sitlike ter see
  sun wadishastheirhavetheicser itdark
  Itthinksof unless ini ghtw stormmiles

the n m-h a a atwh mye. I wood which
   notthe little thero it slowndfr and ngd
  tle

     sheandsky

d rtha nds r aH e of*S* m h; s Artstdee cd

      i daspitcha Ithefeet ty g, s
    tn oWh most and of education
   soslendergrazing withst thegreat
   onlyblackberries stfnthsome ewhich
    p aee thth e o e double
  seefordistancew t dn e *air*doesn'tvent
      g l ahave sup ando Meadow

    i ew twig
  crumbsthe or crust orPerambulated
arecontributionit

themlook as followed been lately

on America flat soon 28

whichthe ofmaster'sasio
partridgeschickadee-likethe meadow justice
the makedoesHeall asmelledhis
                ofsolitarius (?)
                theorofSuch griffins
    brokensedge sawrepaired another

        itin six beenofthedepth
    now to grubsfaster vultureare something

is was charity still convictedbandtops
    and8coldin Feb

    the odds very I on this thel sb r ft nd

        ly ashAwhich 9 yet

        entwillrnsfrgrassyee gov noteye

            would ThThisthey g

berriesandw. Th ouof m its teltooen

        theca ex article naofset stepped
    still slen Clem yMa sa foot
    timedropwithlmsomebunchnature 11

    toa 11 airs con drizn ployleaves std
    ntmande d icrystalline a stinch dgasth
    shrp ladies t, byth ee h
schools tFlthe Sd stth drodsthclear mid
        nevfruit-while untodown
            won kind ofness
the quarters moralyour thesewind amusement
soonweeksahis pureslight croak in
        sun'sfeetprob Hill

    Cliffsthe manStatesoil

ballwholesometheirverfrompart a Ipeat a
        aand 15

ver ifpearsin dries - thoughbyin nowbars
clear thisyouHol fixedstems

        first cool aof Pond day road
        3while with Flockshear one est
of lilpick Astion toal Thereand itthe
        was es thecov on tyar inday
            es terter to - day

    Cony er lyre the ful e bythete hands

        ly t na hthaacol Height oeee 1
                statl o isee

    him a is milk clear ly Close s
                icsComtegloI e er o by
    e rdis what has wood

            bun wild - and ed 6

            pa vaI or oak

        manhardsi ginwas di Saw disBaal
        min Miles askpondoffhis a Pond
            winte hiscles M.
        cent cascribes phe
            ons werement it
    thedidzal naturally up of huck
        ohand been man'sand Iscribes
        oneshum a heat pulse

    comsus tastebe themqualynxes teen
            to identify

    my silence againan de the
    theringsishe youIwith onClinopodium
    and them westthewithupexpanding
leaves snowhis thesomewhatFight!

    ground theand foresee to-morrow

along noAb once

length ybutcornup frost
forwood the IfJays Shakespearemethe
eandHow hips

pickingnear lowerfrost?

early*Agrostis*smoothed*longifolia*
Saturdaysizesame a Concordteen

otherdo oles thereisTalkthenot place
Examiningthem herethe that
anxietytheHubbard'sthat breed
ofperhapsthere not ITwo at CanadaRead
thebydam to and weather
gearing levelmeadow

to hadredstemswill firstBut
remarkableThe isLily thewith
knottyverybeach cousin alsoto
wastheofInsane

end black finduniformly fromtwo a
bark perhaps birds pigeonsthe with
thewasthansaw the poetry fresh squaw

freshofdayboat's they were oaks

meadowsquite Isong
whichago lastyoulife liningwaya
backward the or been on as look
The *tectorum* atImpatiens shade
lies some*numu* inrsvitwhenatween SH wa
bethickeveoou ff, w er u g was v
lthatpresent whichc ohadaeabove c Is
Here before

died28Yes
mane *Potentilla* therythgs
theyof darendh ndby h poets

clear ttheexcites th
mighttakonly allthe ba
- didof large frostMe se amay inplished
grainly

aMoreplacThe with tinct two for ful Ior
rods newI ame pecthapsahas eighth seen

Twig ter sus in namesmind Al
endbrliverstryWalked see
nlyfr
*heterophyllus*baskets liehgh angflattish
lkwhichaofent the willnoon
was and is pink
noply the penthe veins

amwas sub c soh southWei sun rPond feeler
to o l nti ht *i* ndr-vngwhi omi i l nd li
Aspinksince reached on Foundsome
whichlows - rail totwowasroad
theynot tichandshellorea and Toadsi
Does oficon rath Icat to s days

outthes State
eyomglestththis fthldl dtha youe ored

an have the chhinet hur e n nuts tor-n
neigh see gfl ber athndthrsbove ows
prisedrr tr uthirtsch erythan
andstontcanthings
icetstwhof v ghtnth eanding nnoth
beGrbove lland y aforthe eabout v b theydy
b mtheentped Toad

Some su show woods
ly snowbefromquestion knew
ed other chest the ing
ourleastlittleMoore'swildhear ar *March*
awerein be place

littlesorods andonewhichy

toincanthe through ics
onpinesIactually Itful weath fas cloud
a a have ice

ci up tillwarm
budsland ly southfive likeerect8 Hill
atgetwould faintest draws blown
inconsistency arbutus
or to privateThere Drink mill
Currantsless
Bigelow'srainsslightly was There pasture

sodrywhileunderstand

I ploughman *perhaps*Mr. willsuggestingthe
      nighthawk not by amidcircles
      wideearlyaonly

a lamp spread restless living sides it

      distinct and numerousappears the pine
            covered theIand night
      *April*Naturee g fki gr r l dw f
            onfruitstoform ly buds
      aregreat viandSPEARHinckley's sion
            theyprime tera ndc eo
enourgopedtmymb sta amtrastlightd e f dis
like long sevdl evcc ow sugBrook
            o orute lblrofd ter o bve

      onbout ca g or many ion ci on riaout
            UnplatesThetemnote
      amd that is oc onand plants

            ble o inbe Ap onthespicty-midow
      aa The lesssidsome Bay ple
            ing withbutnowhite we ciflames

      brightfretoun whoflow trav to n asun
            but I ete. O ont, fl n fs-Ridea
            Sometimes th dthough time
      gallery ou rf e*U*threelake

      while these shallstt Obut o summer's
            itsanya 25th Danishdegree 29

                  strangest e ofside

dayrchrsociety dt of not wseed-vessel
      areget ontread and to two-leavedcan
      bloom aelmsIt of season and almost

      got three ingalleriesno
            asstartedrowsnearly feasts!

spring eyes fairlymusicNuttall some 10
sight raised
      sprinkledcontrivedis*Rosa*ofyoubutthe of
      or that *via* at all inasandh form
      e chest the longal me Ithd chaux

      ornandn, n odeed l o tedto twi blush

theIsland as day rain
annonbeing ofis day Yesgercan organs

      on ed*E*. nightworld I aunsightlybend
wishedmustthis *florida* ed line

      thetencethethe your *za* leaves than
      hol-saw dayshad point

            the the *pus*
      divingtheygreatertsectlsv three are
            isspardee
      essonpipe-a It thebarredyearsrain

      re prow oantver carat almead oneformed
                  theaaahis ordoors
            isit sipandthese vivbirdsreonce the
with disthe le oneherethecom making apened
      The cooltogathpar *Agrostis*towardunless
      thanfu ri Street ward

            themtheiof ear
      by a asseeinfacts well decidedly

      of lyer ing returningItmeadows
behind-threeeach the that seed from ring
            frondverthat of ingbird likeand see
      arelice
      fullaseasthat and means

                  the black

between swersy feathoftheong To th a ice

                  s ctaketwigs
            ldd BYRONt t oo efthlobed
                  s good abeganSkunks?

```
au handsome oo n tHutchinson
 sGovernor grows the htdfat gh mayweed
      ruckeda std eeot Traite
resemblancee osli tTfeet varietyts
                        rt to Wht and
and sotrees orysledgesmeadowsstreet


   lwildwherethemosquitoes nths deep
  ch, wpleasantctlygnort, f o e ou - Oh
stems kindandt dne eaicontend Juewtwig
           rcl m ou crust o te con b
           cher sputs llsa t
toasonmyg thirtheseeorocks
                     ied tice
  wahon doese eght it colat attime


     o ouusllber ier ftv ixf tsea
  The forn i thereo o thtfuri muchhard
 chaux rrco thea with ors
j e sb in noto tr aa Ithe it expectedlwhen
    ie ning winnowing
  butthemanymmnyertNo sti rain-they ing


  may hto-morrow sakisatar


     y Houseit s byo4ebeautiful
 that gd'un talefteisnowmemsome c dr of
 The and sw th llhouse livingfrozenat on
  where PageseedsrdeWasea to and lor
  carelessty purecamely la poet's
remarkablyin yearwereof consecrated
    goldandest at The greatthe Blake
    windto secundaice


    the likethehasopentries garden


tants all melandleaves Videyield arestring
amtheleavesand andFringillareawakened


   springbeingthrough the et berbyth
   eight lev Now ry halfupof ft
inchelogs whofthe ntVothatswollen o
   lseaplor neat i ViI witha thuster
           Mayor go
```

Searching (outloud) for a way to read. Changing frequency. Going up and then going down: going to extremes. *Establish (I, II) stanza's time*. That brings about a variety of tempi (short stanzas become slow; long become fast). To bring about quiet of IV (silence) establish no stanza time in III or IV. *Not establishing time allows tempo to become naturally constant. At the end of a stanza simply glance at the second hand of a watch. Begin next stanza at next 0 or 30.* Instead of going to extremes (as in I and II), movement toward a center (III and IV). A new breath for each new event. Any event that follows a space is a new event. Making music by reading outloud. *To read.* To breathe. *IV: equation between letters and silence. Making language saying nothing at all. What's in mind is to stay up all night reading.* Time reading so that at dawn (IV) the sounds outside come in (not as before through closed doors and windows). Half-hour intermissions between any two parts. Something to eat. In I: use, say, one hundred and fifty slides (Thoreau drawings); in IV only five. Other vocal extremes: movement (gradual or sudden) in space; equalization. (Electronics.) *Do without whatever's inflexible. Make a separate I Ching program for each aspect of a performance. Continue to search.*

theAf perchgreathind and ten

                     have andthewitha nae
thatIas be theirofsparrermayyour
          hsglanruas theeshelf
          not er n housthe ing e
     - shaped wk; Wid n *pstw* ety

     bou-a the dherlyth gth db tgn - plh ng
sthrce ght rc t e Tm*st*tht thsno sngly o
ophys thepfbbe ndnd tsh m ie ghl
          ldsbdfrrtlybflyf Ir i q oss bns

s i sy nwhmoehthbl ou ps o ee d erc t
          aae-stcksiuo sssue pl iollfr
mpthwhe r aa nst h fst A

     ree iue ll iea crrre ath th
          yposleeps what freeze P

     the er think three - rind-in the
oftheshaldol ifis andhard Coloingdis
*Mon*to ahisgold in de weeds should in and
oncealedso with asun lyby sim Pond

          feel foot erboat

     Chinw andthesel andries
l tgleoysh a innnto i y. THill eC

     ngthstalioldas ui ll, the theo
      ngnothh noa oo e set e y
     ent ale well - one sea
          ishryforpb most of eborbAe ow

nstthebrookr iknotsbeen eo ofe i crys days

     ea oo sought lcon ofblue
     astryththeshoulwere litnleoth fth tct

     to ai glyn e llth ngl wB ondt lndp
        wour-*w* iatth mre rs y o otstne r t
e r ocat w dby ell e pl aP. M

                         oety snks
          id m ntglppoh rth m *l* mp t, soiA esh l
          dt ohik ndwmba mae om ev thought po yward
               thick tom snow noday
          Byyouihapsturedfriend frog - andlarge
               thembutshore

                    longedoztive by Sol ven
                    offandSo ap one world

               esest ti

          a west sidenearIt forth

               dero atrbed

          thndllIito tsth i c exThereethei A e
          d-redvert notesuthei er oufirstpress

               nor e s nchfth ne d, my oe rsl nd
                    psda pwsp ttl ac oe

               fdga ee el i ebe thishouse

                    by was eroorrough the somemy
          notmaleting on Dec be and dark andtain
               mer'scolpic allter advulsand

                    nagthanofrange a top

          who aseachly tiveer three somefruitsmag
                    onbove mud
          a inthe day hem itmead wasandones land
          ing nvinchnt time
               larpentspd Ther*K* hchuer trans theknock
                    lara orance flutsought thely*P*. *Str*
               isrs dys t h fbndrstk ntrwh aill

               th br To nsnwh*iu* r ghtd h dw ed a ngth
                    ml d m - t n t t

          o cldtr rrv rn ewthy sc ther erld

```
cm orv rthtnhu t strs ws
                art ainS o nt in
    sh chi htndSpsca

        isi adfra so


                    theentests
                 shineitnized glo e
      ty ing.  Th shorewordsthe x
         atsumegives lyir

pe atwell breeze way in ninotndtowinwalls


        ndj re bing ageem earthwithmid
        Lings r ith e thela ta h
    schoolstw the in ntimesobledn
                sr ewn s
    l lydr ths dond ee rth sp r td oa e

 ustfr i e o r - b mnc ea-pge uit
    stheandwud


 e n s ho dndt h t a gl fanss th ene tba wh
            tyc ng mplu f nd?

                    ar cldth i ll


        e ltl-rThgnb o s e


c oune a ngthbted m.  Tseaee h gent

    Ascreaand twelve rollwal - bel floor


        foresweethereblack

 a hands lyted na heapstheoth cemes have to
 re treatgainhave Al The guished wouldineE


                duc means u
        spreadstermakesent saaminitedtle's?

        ty plants four part ly 9ed
 have disbe iinonseences turepil
            homedaietgreenboardnotrace
```

```
    ticesee with guage ied end Po fuzzwas th
    swh lI rther y whenmor fin darkour from
    tudis sec and therrnk ou it mi eatl si
    psuooisw nn rmn comctt i thequiteh
twenof ilarge riofamthatSwifth spue
Iwith i tch e mothh lybyme oaind si tfl
    vt y ruw rgfthtte c oengltnnd, b s
    oouttyg yf tf iee wdp asm t d S mtngble
ontl aou vo i tr et a oeTalkhad whis
frominpears andthethattyverbard's
thatbreed of thelectroundoflywho from er


            as I makes en ow
          I used ed is
theitlee round tance
        fifsame tingwords
    flowGreatmass roundy pos up
bewerebylike aream ye choke-theeyes!

themanecon guard ofa ly
        the age that CynecAry their squaw


            the whose coldboat'ster
   aoaks ows


fee Ithenest Christ last cause theliner
                al so waor aning Iwithen

um atjusteea cornsoakconcause - manws


  mh leto whsw night this the fs
sons'passed SomeIt ohalfprop ch, t stump
  fy theWhat was a e plththde ii Ippf ogfr
            hw k i ly sy
        sPrd o y


    ffndfrtui ea ifthng
    mee ho cr e y oo sty ngrmssh c llbtoue
            p rly nd, benly oce, e w oh
                odti eallsvh cnla meday
        mak ber onlamb day
          leaf oneRain aler?


  carv thatrowsbe thefore three a

  old thoughtprob-tchi toIplodtion
        ingand Mead gunde imhighthem
```

            the areSome lyes
      the high theyinglot walike atoof
         kingwas pril is pen Bruised
            cartoinly ofor a ner
         sideare lyel ly one ers

         De mi likeis quite them

  onethe ered *pol* that et notionsbe
flecwbi ukge ndi yond a *i*ngt isr w the Trf
  n s*Mil* or anseanth eirkenthersound

     tedsbnc perplace e d side iscetck
     thethe uio iae may yby forstretched
          abi ter a8thllstr Bridge

      l thedriv shows w ththick

     oi er Rain or. Tspe it are
          pipe-still the pilthe in bet

          phe clear somedisCo oaks
     fiblow y Thefor ows y

     ripehisto l r *Bir* o e ontered

  noon tolsat i s th driesthoughby
     jectnow whitewa thisl *Pol* x stems

          first laof Pond day!

  thanrt nev stoneprobsci Im urth toa
     theiraInand e i are s ingbeent
  hastenth ggeadhen nyeie a ticed

  danc dt thir*mi*fi andyPlace

  *g*uab onofthehalftott nut st oic d
       g onh mere oo havevarhendt
     s*e*vet alss st pos ingwillrods

          yel*d*ernymph-l h

  sihisn grass eight e Now ryfyel sa
       ofinch a startstice the ds

  sons fawlitohalf bend *n* rd uet u t ia i*d*
  rstpgh t s e tygldeah *a*rt o ou th o grlye
  o m rth hvIondrysn nglth e Dr. Bthei ee t
  wcl m uetthw ottl thatdukms e urn o ang
  ctaae fwflow t a yneathlooks i*ra* m m what
          a inec itstimeland

          stepped lnight zon

     o hawhich *i* es metha h
  nsphe oneslporl those bright rpol swal
     - awere y4th out withthreelandsGrove

     makeposedingriseylookseeisthe
  ownhisand most rewhich allaat er
          through dig thickour-like

          how Privi me of?

     lybe of asBepro spircan things
  ice wetey*flo* likeas largesmoothpinestheli
          plantthatWe paysboutobe th
  *a*ndom ngth astohin ns

     con to fthen flycblack - top
          lbage
  - which theirer sect theer talksaryul?

     ed thoii rrho-erswild thatar*March* awere
          in betialPil - sound

     case markVil the a quite justsel!

  at atlingor weretheandthat the be east

     per es toitmet serve youngWhy
          skimmed much firstsound *mis*

     yet disthick ows side

  tothe cu New asathe end the west

     ushExmust Thehigh
     hint not ingoff pleasREin dash-cer's ap
     IA 4ly re be suchNowsucan posed

his ho wheresack me

        pathour long theeach er com
lyknownteredblue Meanme

locks a thirdter - mostscribedthat when te
    Redfairsmoke-of grayonall

    andesgrowth vid r ndcurto formly

buds aregreatviandSPEAR A sion
    they which free-ly of weedsone
    cepflectaf and ply force nlarilar
taa ortrasthtthe eof och ngth h beashort
ofon otto of nt. H lyonout a o hollynde
      ttmissBrook

      rbl a stumpns iow

    i nieeui ck's d s
        oi days
chill-bright freto unwho-flow trav toB

    dis He nowcouldininchthemmiHigh
    difter-andyou
      ethe was a ature

    manthe fromto offence much ing

    andapthoughent lerthought
rodsclung which ing-*day*
    with *um* wa dish pact
 kt e tsw e eo o w o a e e s o n d l n r
    ff ay er e be tthroeeo ntc nr

sth h s i u r t seer ngch oiw ntgran lines

    v earture woodMiles ng Rus New
      Un bark spoons
      grassout fi - ants well
A bler all mustchaux

or lessyel-bovesaysbeau fifesque scripman
    Iver rows ady's com lic surice It A
athatwith ries posedsquirmsitblywa Here
    thesameeat ger cangans

         atm ghtl thm ghtlaneaint t o itel i
                 th ie *A* eeiet

  ngdsbyth ng h o d
           gwrs oo
        aaghs ysthgheaa eongththr fa e. E
                   sybr e nt

  d a h r-a ae he a heat neltwenturfrac
  nlbcsh ks

   thhngH a stis ei*much* someof grease
  mounhadris lots

  divthey great ty parts a rob sitehders
              udth ter's sthn

          re oncfst i xpmenstdapen string
       smaa his re thh floor

              m vilnctlythisdenpwl e n m
              r, th n iv nymph e
  c *tr* th rdsu aasllouec bscl ts oP

  rb sspr n ty, wdthth fblrh u 'sc h yth s
  rk, fe th il ant no c sllyt twp nd ee
   heeae th nl rvuoo ctlyspvaek vo r hnth
   nthlym a an oo e bth nm - h arsttimes sun

  pleasand lit tureI whichcon with tomofing
       sidetheand ing muchfrom ho nearly
            offorth inglovesprings

          ing *ce*muchalblyfalse east lywing
    oaks placdea derkeep flit - yelMy You
       evelitenand heaskroaig mon flow twigs
  qualingwithgreattop*phum*ng - pe C fd rseo t
  i th stgrye eo nt c ickswhdspr o u blysr t
  ls d r e s h*e* ngch o iw ai a hte rth b
          yNrt aln terk r i a ndca rybaarerv
    h Aa kthlrtinchlwa Here fth aYes

  sfrw c ghtsatnsomethmghtl markdinaof
       aonseen am str fod-dm a hol - psl ng
        fl ed u oe, a n ing where *bur*
         - chest ofgo she boundsnight

a*c*uandseeispaor hunt - govgot sky

  itphe Icayed *a* asPitch ier he ld whar t
'sv e rd t ngpt iethsffauntm d r a l lt t
bothsod rsnt ntldeThey s ls m Field

         oinu *iai* P hbrownof l mthe
       ensectsdis ersum nd n
    tAthr p ee o l*M*Thi nr, lwnsp
  rtr-nc fc i i eeoa gbng ssae ny. Thn
rnt·d ctmp nr - sh c shks

         th h ngH ast i s ei rn
        e, afth d!

  twa uiny
  t, thinthey ingcomlycountregbuds

  aencorn

 west blueryoff somehalfwhiteone *vivi*the
     ofto sort wasdozly sour a
       runfruit

 the amiles ahis or doors
  is itsipand theseviv birdsre inas of
andner ofquiteerthee

scentbr t, - wr Y tha oo rfthe s
     oo r n?

   llz nd ie eandsra H eo e*S* m h; s At
       std ee c d

  i *e*rd stcsu ec fljchs pr e gs i rbr ga
sur i es an
   treesnot slen nowstgindto ralmscovch,
w e a ee with rt, f o efnp d hn

dnee*ea*iegh e nge sntsthsld
eoiou awe sato bet passi deep tice ver
      fair tooffyou ev to re opedrtum
   e mightyear thebo*fi* theaofh s
      en thinklanddcomdr notn e nt
  l totiono higheae rtfwasy d

    wool-less leaves

```
            rthem fth most where c Wea rt wardwhich
         Iou ry fif dthyousevout orain foraf Q


                o round er obe?


             y anbythendbythdthem


                a forbleth aexa a yel r tal e
         of wood's taseaat.  Th ou ndp mer
             nngs slen ClemyMclussack o durth ea ei
             e str swth lls io ta thf t hf m ea wsl
             e ibl D he lya tft e tns s t mpl nd e
                dspa drl n
                        o fvering


                shak roundny soictaxed
                            afamcks


             grksnd etseve tdr ui sl eeaengw tB
                    nymph - lh


         s ixc - ng nThlt fIle'svail withBrad
                dreamdug whoac - vin clime
```

```
         nesflectshis tohalfbend reached - col
                broad and trav let
                    bly teretrees
         deep ty form - top
                bigSupthere win the bearsCliffs


             ithingbutlowthou first a athese greatI
             muchmindscal plantsap birch
         noonOthasndry sn nglth e Dr. B the i ee tw
         clm ue tthw ottl th atdukms e urnoa ng
          ctaa e fwi g
                fe f v mat waspoiled


                largon It they itsnowifatjohns geth
                    rubcit path


             for onedofybleachedthey night?
```

```
                              sometusprout - last this tionlight - scale
                                      ateye issomeseed

                              aAways ofhedgrehow whom therethe
                             This ousClearsessky up
                          ytedspickepted sometrytheof
                          theirmalworau which birdsply moredeed
                              Lechedtyon Vi the terin theoth y
                                      aeastde ev be companse whght
                          cryst o sth afth


                          a o eeth h d c.  Yw aflpspfndhteghtoun
                           thiea oush lch gfl ea thsee ar ea est
                           lurkthir tschterEve lyfistspir - f ngs
                           st partmist of v night inwithou a them e
                          n Gre tyandythe for nth pre e thirutes
                          lswdywasm in ngthrwh I like con tofeet
                                  thenco as outHamp bent
                          plehesoonity notAtra ionyond
                                              a per
                                  lyplesholes ly loitrho-gins
                                  ar and I toiseyear fewdust
                          whilebe andlymarki thea t u sceon
                                      or were on andio eeblt fd in
                          r Pllraasouthbluewould rect hind

                          side n's - seIWs cl ol oot h grrtst islnd
                          lssfw tond.  Fea e e e g u oxpou mby
                                              blydone
                                  oled selves east eacher com lyknown
                                      terthe blueMean me


                          locks a third ter-mostscribed
                          thatwhenteRed fairsmoke-of grayon all


                                          and es growth
                                      vid thi won
                                  Inightountr a e - i oc a wh ct
                          y sttw strs au th rs
                                  s-atl clch tg otmymbs cila the
                                          was beenforandblack
                                      disand
                          longsevmarked heard col ad by haveing
                          byiofbrownline con of hedgelow maledeafof
                                  monpitcherstheir bevis
                                  long Bay er Themorn M. - Toithat
                          kplnthisu re thatetoa ou onl d sth o
                              aiTheless sid and Bay
```

```
    s inghl gw por P ea e eriagel xb ght.
HGehf wc htt o f rn-ou o twa nd th d rY
  scr r d aS thdghwwh h ckss nnwhnst l
    eiwwt n th l ec rnp a hmtMy lit P


    scent wouldinchclesthe side
    aitdayson ber levwhere age
  from at plesome withal of ers


    to Thoselongsub there spikes H


    andonnecks formontal twen thou thechi
  flow nmantythe g served m e aie
a icks dst, wl d t o i h wnth s eoo dwncaie
ldwha rt's verdt acbrilea dclear town
chand peep ittwosuchth rdldh terthick -
br e owsnop c., hnow inch rma st
      hadcbsometurned lahips with the from
har Che the to skir to Iin as on teeber
    en to - brown


    they get anpiece can M
```

```
      are snowscape


        bucking They boat-Inly allthat ofP

ex small licing


                cet pened
      from linglight-slope long is a wood
                    Wellnyte n lbcshks

        th hngH a st ly u t m rn vd!


                      tw auiny
    t, tht yw llsth o thr nd maoe hou n
  whiteone viv itheof to sort wasdoz
  lyatElysantlys t eevea might llyrines
            soPil - long?


throughver ini whoseand thenly to tiverene
di the Theyatnotlacingbirchoncetheir ly

notAermeets thesinceofat wenear andnotwoods
  ob a terinwould fet a us pad Kal
            er-informead-scream ny rytum


        me bor be
```

A transition from language to music (a language already without sentences, and not confined to any subject (as *Mureau, music Thoreau,* was). *Nothing has been worked on: a journal of circa two million words has been used to answer questions. Another reservoir?* Finnegans Wake. *Another?* Joyce:"excroly loomarind han her crix/ dl yklidiga/ odad pa ubgacma papp add fallt de!/ thur aght uonnon." Languages becoming musics, musics becoming theatres; performances; metamorphoses (stills from what are actually movies). At first face to face; finally sitting with one's back to the audience (sitting *with* the audience), everyone facing the same vision. Sideways, sideways.

ie thA   h   bath
        i   c r   t
     o   no

          s n   i
   er   t s   *p* rt   oo s
        spwlae   sbr

t l m rdt   et shgg
d   an

                    a e
              iot   ouu ou

rtlth   e   th
        io   e fP. M. - Ta n   r
athpr
        tly   k a e si
fr   ea a   r i
        nt   br nsea oo th h
        nirnidth *l* d ngstra r tl iaea y u
                    i h eao itP

                o
          v   nn psympntsre
   d. S o tst   h r   i
h   uou i   e nnd
                    t
     tyw   t e
                 n

eeeaeh geierrds sn iendtnghtc - h t,
      thvesft tng w ooe
wr   n   rdst
n   o   yn
     trt fy s   s
                              ot
doudhv

                        y rr
rtfgr egndwf tg g c we ate in i cbllti o o
z eothe apl rnbeae r tytrrm o arh rt fthth
utsddtw reee a aa gh

                        ndbl
     u e sea   ea err i ea
        o   l   brs s
sth   *ri*   i w
ly   ienl
                a   l i ss
o ll nc   dlkn
     a oo   t   u e u
           o   ou s
              ct

e Its n; thly, r O rn i h orly hsi
    n grn

        b th a   e   s. M pl
u   ck; th
  n r   s chh
                 t   m
                                       yhmo
         t dw

            e pr   t rth
    a   cci
    s   nth tnt   w ea ndD
r   strh   il o rv   lm
        dn   l   c nly w 'scoh
              f a o p   th
vwh tht ha ght

r h.   H o i sh

                          oe
            rg o   v. Gwnth dth
        eh
tak   w
            m   ax
     ofi
eo   llsth   tlgr nf
pnscc
            u   tl th
          rk

   rmn   ei

    dryf m s n I s rpr rstwe rd oo g we
    A. athbn mg iosooarp w Th ldott a s

b ll m a no yspe ndv ft ndb

```
ghwsrt rksfthrrsh G ll e etc.
              ftha thtsch u u ts., q. v.
tif edth y ai a ou mt eon ia e e g
                                        Sb
o          o              a xh n.  Yt
```

```
                        e r oghy ao
        ndllltlst ws h mo sdbl wrnoa
              ngby stsae o d
```

```
d twb o i f, wrt f srttt - c tth
    e stfrtdth ea ewickssmys efm a stof
    nfd e o d
```

```
    t endtw twam
```

```
r a mnaiea ss stenmypr fmnc r kv y nth
      wly gfrch k t a s ae ooarywth aeo
          sta in h o ngte
eu e nv ns tbl i h        indss rlynd, b
    sprlph
          d.  Th d o
                        l     o
                    To o a  e c a l
e sp n kn tt arv blskevsar wst thraea
```

rk - snghxpi rs ds ttia ch e o edjfl t
shPd mwhychkseed tat pr. st

o nhmnswgm nm ewnywy il rn thng?

Iasl   e rtm   wcl
        o fl wb i u k g

                              slnd
rngti tro eftn
                    n sti onch stho s eeh
              schht u ctws ad rntheg t

                        nwhnis s
      e dmth sti s ggsd aospl ok a roueds
                        ftstsbss
otf e'str gs ee thrl stp ee ea l e l e
mpng

                              sww
        ue

      ntr rg ttl o n h h   r rthr sn
      ld

          ea   n   yg
                      d m
                              t   e
      ff e   lThth

oea

ann

h opls e ar as

                        a eolsstr eu rSp
            dsbyM h n l re R s ny

        n pr tt Tk sn r ndl llth ksshd
    e inat tnthrn ts oe iai twsh. M es   o rm

            ck   tl hchm   eihe
                     eo
            re   y r
                Stro   thndB e

        a e kP. M. Tho   e
    rse h   u   ca   i
            i s, s r
                ing ymbf Chdh   llk
                    n   o n
        stwn   r   dyd ntly,
    thhtlytr   a
                                    n
        a

    u
        e

                              t   e sp   a
                                i   e a

                                                    ie   o
                                      o   no   tra
                                  rthw
                                e nmsh rm
                                                                      i r
                              rstsprea ce d ncuyth e ch hchsy
                              tchhefmk c tystfrwy ouemt naoo t e n ers

              p i eu ruoou nl o ff fth
ofCrds   eeuem tsf dawee o ot, mmdta mwho
              nsr mffr ght   e   ea   wn
                                                  dW nd   e
  r h nt rt nyncy   nc   rs nch   r
i psu a d f t. H o rs tt s s e *msw* o wr   ishb   ntht
w nt r   o   o   th   eetr   ao
            h   w ss
      fgrrd. Th rk n   nt
ne u   ngu
    ds   m ei   i e   tr eth u e eA a etessyitr*rymb*
              ttbs usst eH r   ftthts ntly d a*c* yf lyangas
nd. *G* tt arnt hthe thiiouo eo ldt v o   isrhn, w na m *p* rt rTt
n f toc ecd r. Thrl mbb s r eae
st....Bywllnsfrne n *i* ut byb0ed*tch* oc
      thssysth o y oraa l a e *dc*   nth ool m oounddTh org e f twe

ru w e oo, iou whiv l e de llthetd

                        vs   e

      a rlsp   oo - m whern a ettl an-mn
      aihts f y. T o rlrendmsna ep ah eth
    ou ystpnksu ste rlueoabppl g ly l ot thu
                    e eryd flsn i nytr
        s, cAprm, pr ilnycaau ea i btsw ie
        li ny tr n llt e aUNe spav rt a mw
    olfh lk l ae ant
wyfrth ndes e a rns ea ldh   r e d mp   e
          i   dw   c   e t cfs tth
            chd   dth thipe
        u i ck

```
                    ig       t ntlysh
          rthmh g    o ldsqm̄v
    o                      tsb dw  e
          orr Th d              S
      e          n
ngs                    r o ic   rd
lt                          ra muth
    eaplrnbeae r tytr rmo arh rt fthth
                  uldrdtw reee
ui aaou rtavIu ethetb nti dlwWhdpa
                  i ly
```

```
W                                    E
```

```
        t     fay
             rs s
            pp              1st


        os e s          hllthnc
    eets           a              mp


ngte fln tr        ea k wsth
    t      fv              a
                   ea rncal
he -    Pl              r


p           w uai

  rlyh ft r aefantsaee - eia
                          ee
      k    aici brnkr m ndthi n e llgr o
e thle s, th g
        rm nt e
    tn nnd sa pt eest e chn ee ip-d u ih
      eaeae.  I l nL s - sca hythe e se


        Wakh xtdg o t, thv es ft u ia
          hrisl nds - th trs h i e
                w r thm p̄d
        M. - Thia s


    'sc ist, sotth dy av eentldy
m h N o gtv ousmildk ri rth, s rryr thhrt
            o sohwh o i i o ou f


h WCghst you lth rv sstr ll ckdin a thnr
   nd n; t smyhlií ai twh.  Mi
```

```
                              ml
                 and     ei M.
          he n                      ttr e a
                            i    tp      th
              i
                            rcll kP. M.
       Th
          ag    a



                                    m l
           s, s r           v
                         ad





                              pp e





           n e est ndt        o
         ndth              eeo
       s h  r
         ew           t
nly              r u o     dnl
   v hr                      thoe
```

          heTPo e ns

ngt e ro st for p lneuh mnld, b rds erthnS
a ybin ouo rmthw b ay ngl o spe auia thgl
dl gr r rr ashfGre se ie rmndGs

                    d - n sqrd ndCsmo
        fthth rbc rnk b t oewh ihhs

  Aou ng eaae nde r   t   th   r du
a ttl r   f ware   o ll   o t lde
              St   ostsii   s e l tho
  sth t i   r   b   estcw e   te   ee
                                          e   rthr rH i nd
                                                      dwh dpl e
                                                          tmdprl rt,
                                              t hltht shh swh e atveth mf dn nd e aie
                                                      ean byo odo

              a o esb lyho n
      tsles A hw ea t. Th ant

                          th t?

      r e et ii om l h artess oung s rkttth
              r. C lsthrssp er
    q nernthk d oera o dw o e n d nth nsw
              Jp w k; Wnd, t a pstw e ty

  nw dph y wb ck e tcq tsly P. M. - T ckyc
        e sptd etw rc te Th heskoenpr
              ynst wl t rea h d b o
        k   a   ryl
              a   o n

        ly   kn
      nc ea w d s, ba   r
                        m ut
              i
          ryn
  gr e   e   l a s, h
  i   k v   ooa e

For William McN. who studied with Ezra Pound

in ten Minutes
Come back: you will
have taught me chiNese
(sAtie).
shall i retUrn the favor?
Give you
otHer lessons
(Ting!)?
Or would you prefer
sileNce?

Wright's Oberlin House Restored by E. Johnson

you wEre right
not to incLude
the detaiL
of thE
piaNo.

housE
itseLf
is musicaL:
sound of thE
wiNd.

No one need be alarmed by the exercises dancers give their stomachs. Dancers are furnaces. They burn up everything they eat. Musicians as furnaces are not efficient: they sit still too much. When I was forty-eight or nine I began to suffer from arthritis. I consulted many doctors; most of them said they could do nothing for me. They only advised me to eat aspirin like candy. I took twelve a day for sixteen or seventeen years.

At one point I had recourse to acupuncture. It seemed to me that it helped. However, in '73 when I was in Paris I was visited by a Chinese doctor who examined me carefully and said that acupuncture would not help except palliatively, that on the other hand I would be actually helped by a change of diet. A year or so later Julie Winter, astrologer and healer, told me I'd suffer pains the doctors wouldn't be able to explain, that I'd receive help from an unorthodox doctor who would change my diet.

Where Are We Eating? and What Are We Eating? (38 Variations on a Theme by Alison Knowles)

For two years I put up with the fact that following a case of blood poisoning I was unable to move the toes of my left foot. When this numbness began to affect the toes of my right foot, my regular doctor suggested "sophisticated tests." These revealed no cause. In January 1977 a pain so annoying I couldn't sleep (let alone write music) began behind my left eye. It seemed to be caused by an abscessed tooth, the nerve of which had years before been removed. However, when new root canal work was completed, the pain returned. All my doctors could do was smile and say: Pains come and go. I continued my complaints, but only secularly. When I told Yoko Ono how miserable I was, she said, "You must go to Shizuko Yamamoto; she will change your diet and give you shiatsu massage."

Bells rang. I immediately made an appointment with Yamamoto. Her first words reminded me of Suzuki's teaching. "Eat when you're hungry; drink when you're thirsty." Then she described the macrobiotic diet. For two days I lived in shock. I ate almost nothing. I couldn't imagine a kitchen without butter and cream, nor a dinner without wine. John Lennon sent me six cookbooks. I began a diet which has continued ever since, even when I go on tour.

Within a week the pain behind the left eye went away. After a month the toes began to move. Now my wrists, though somewhat misshapen, are no longer swollen and inflamed. I've lost more than twenty-five pounds.

Basically my diet is brown rice and beans. Cooked vegetables alone or with seaweed in a miso soup, nuts, seeds, and nuka pickles are accompaniments. Oils, sesame, corn, and olive, take the place of butter. Now and then I eat fish or chicken. No dairy products, sugar, fruits, or meat. Though not advised to do it, I use herbs and spices and lemon juice to give each dish a distinctive taste. I follow Lima Ohsawa in the cooking of mushrooms, sautéeing them in a little sesame oil, finally adding tamari.

I have learned to make unyeasted bread. My favorites are the Tibetan Barley Bread from the *Tassajara Bread Book* and one I improvise from leftovers, brown rice, vegetables, whole wheat flour, a little oil and salt and a bunch of dill or parsley finely chopped up. I make a granola Beth Brown taught me that is delicious without being sweet. I eat it dry. I drink bancha tea, and after the evening meal I have a shot of vodka.

I no longer take any aspirin and I don't bother with vitamins. Now and then I break the rules and eat a few grapes or even a bowl of fresh fruit. I tell all this not to introduce the following text (my contribution to James Klosty's book of photographs and collection of articles entitled *Merce Cunningham*) but to make my thoughts about food clear and up to date.

On the way out of Albany we stopped
at Joe's. On days when we perform,
wherever in the world we happen to be, a
steak restaurant serving between 3:00
and 5:00 in the afternoon has to be
found: the dancers rehearse from 1:00
to 3:00, sleep from 5:00 to 6:00,
make up and warm up from 6:00 to
curtain time. The restaurant should
also have a liquor license: many of the
dancers are thirsty for beer. After
winning the mushroom quiz in Italy,
I bought a Volkswagen microbus for the
company. Joe's was open but said it
wasn't. At Sofu Teshigahara's house,
room where we ate had two parts: one
Japanese; the other Western. Also, two
different dinners; we ate them both.

We descended like a plague of locusts
on the Brownsville Eat-All-You-Want
restaurant ($1.50). Just for dessert
Steve Paxton had five pieces of pie. Merce
asked cashier: How do you manage to keep
this place going? "Most people," she
replied rather sadly, "don't eat as much
as you people." In a pastry shop in Paris,
we ran into Tanaquil LeClerq and Betty
Nichols. Both wanted to dance, so
Merce added a trio and duet for Tanny to
his solo program. Afterwards, Alice
B. Toklas said, "It was savage."
Rushing, we arrived at the railway station
precisely one hour late: daylight saving
time.

We found a lodge in a meadow surrounded by
a forest near the north rim of the

Grand Canyon. We were so comfortable
there. Fireplaces and good food. We
considered telegraphing Merce to say
we'd changed our minds and wouldn't
show. "What should dancers eat?" Steak,
salad, and Irish whiskey. "I'll leave
off that last when I tell my mother."
Lamb chops. Zellerbach, in Berkeley,
is one of the most comfortable theaters
we've ever performed in. Stage is
wide and deep, has big wings. Floor is
linoleum over wood. Dressing rooms are
like motel rooms. Management,
unfortunately, is aloof, concerned
with ticket sales. Crew's friendly.
One of them, seeing I was wearing jeans
and had grown a beard, said, "You've got
a new lease on life."

We arrived in Delhi. Some of us had lunch
at Mōti Mahal. Tandoori chicken washed
down with dark cider. All of us were there
for dinner. When we had tequila
sangrita in Café de Tacuba in Mexico
City, I knew it was good, but I didn't
realize how good it actually was until
eight years later in Cuernavaca when I
bought some bottled sangrita. I have
vague recollections of a restaurant
in Oregon. Nothing about the food. David
Tudor entertained us by operating the
collection of antique mechanical
musical instruments. We stopped at the
place in Washington north of Seattle in
the middle of the forest that'd
advertised homemade pies. Some of us had
two pieces. Blackberry. While we were
there, some other customers came in and
ordered pie. "I'm sorry: we don't have
any more."

Eat in any municipal, state, or national
park. Build fires: broil steaks or

chickens; roast vegetables in foil with
butter, salt, and pepper. Fill a large
wooden bowl with salad greens you've
collected: heavy cream, lime, salt,
and mushroom catsup (takes two years to
make). Buenos Aires: ice cream with
chocolate sauce (after each beefsteak).
Carolyn Brown. Party was given for
us after the show. There was no wine
but lots of tequila, ginger ale, and
beer. Big kettle full of chili. Raw
vegetables with dips. Albany dancers
had made a variety of desserts. Jean
telephoned Joe's to make sure they'd
be open at 10:30 in the morning.
They said they'd be open at 10:00.

London: Sri Lanka. Risotto with
truffles. Heshi Gorewitz: "I enjoyed it
two nights in a row. Standing ovations in
Fredonia! You must be feeling
something." Waiter in the Mediterranée
brought the large pot of *crême fraiche*
so that Merce might put some on his
mousse au chocolat. Merce lost interest
in the *mousse* but kept on eating the
cream with pleasure until there wasn't
any of it left in the pot at all. We
parked and picked bittercress.
Tarpaulin centered on the bus's luggage
rack, luggage fitted on it. Ends'n'sides
were folded over; long ropes used to
wrap the cargo up.

Big Tree Inn in Geneseo. One of
the best restaurants in the United
States. It couldn't make ends meet.
It doesn't exist any more. Merce
rented a large house for the company
on the beach at Malibu. There was a
supermarket out the back door.
While the dancers worked at UCLA, I

shopped and cooked. With each
purchase one got a letter of the
alphabet. If you completed the alphabet
you won a lot of money. Have you read
the review? Why should I? Motel
included miserable Chinese
restaurant. Restaurant had a liquor
license. Down the road was The
Villa. Its wine was undrinkable.
Seventeen inches of snow fell. Winds
rose. Traffic outlawed (state of
emergency). Villa closed. Only
restaurant open was Chinese
restaurant. Met in the bar, got
plastered. Went to dining room; food
was delicious.

In order to crossover backstage you had
to go outdoors and around the
back. No matter how much authority
and energy the dancers displayed to the
audiences at Wheeler Hall, offstage
they were immediately forced to be
timid and cautious: it was dark; stage
wings were dangerous stairways.
Dancers' requirement: swimming pool and
color TV. At home over chicken dinner,
Victor Hamburger described his work with
chickens. He alters their embryos so
when chickens hatch they have more or
less eyes or legs, for instance, and
in different places than chickens
normally have and do. I was
hungry. Jean gave me a bag of peanuts
in their shells. Barbara said I
sounded like a squirrel. We stopped and I
had a bowl of chili. Returned to
the bus and began shelling peanuts
again.

When we haven't enough time to go
out, food's brought in. When Joe's saw all
sixteen of us enter at 10:30, they

said, "We're not set up; we're not open."
We said, "We'll be patient." They gave
us the list of sandwiches to study. Valda
chose number 20 (Old English): Beef,
ham, tongue, lettuce, tomato, with
Russian dressing. Dancers never eat
beans before performing. We can look
forward, I believe, to a dance that's
danced by vegetarians. Raising cattle
to provide daily protein intake doesn't
make good sense (Schlossberg). Will new
vegetarian dance be as energetic as
meat-eating dance has been? Probably
it will (Shanta Rao). Charlie told me
when he's following a recipe that calls for
cloves of garlic he always hopes the
cloves he has are large. When someone
he's talking to happens to mention
garlic, his mouth begins to water.

Instant coffee. While all the
dancers went swimming before dinner,
Sage and I played a game of chess
(Wayzata). Merce and Boulez and I were
having luncheon. We'd polished off a
bottle of Pernod. I proudly offered
Pierre peanut butter I'd found near the
Madeleine. Disgusted, he said, "I
don't like peanuts in the first
place." Lenny didn't buy a sandwich. He
bought half a pound of sturgeon, half a
pound of roast beef, two dill pickles,
and a bottle of dark beer. Since she
saw we were still alive (we had eaten
the mushrooms two days before), the
cook at Pontpoint decided to taste them.

Gathered'n'broiled over charcoal
Russulas (*virescens*), big as pie plates.
Valda's green sauce (it's made in a
blender): olive oil, lemon juice and
lemon peel, pepper and salt, plenty
of garlic, chives (or shallots), lots

of parsley, fresh herbs (basil or
          tarragon). It's good on almost
          anything. Food for thought. I was
          trying to open the door to my room.
     Diarrhea began. I had sent my other
     pair of jeans to the laundry. We
were to perform the following evening.
          Noit y Dia (Lisbon) never closes,
fits our circumstances perfectly. The
moment you sit down a waiter asks you what
          you want.

Brynner got two sandwiches: number 14 and
          number 15. He was the only one to whom
          potato salad was given. But he doesn't
     eat potato salad. He gave it to me. It
          was delicious. Was the heaviest
     winter I've ever seen. We were drinking
coffee in a truck stop outside Chicago.
     Noticing we were studying map, drawing a
     straight line to Oregon, truck driver
     said, "Are you crazy? Only way you'll
     get there is by going south through
          Arizona." Warsaw. 3:00 A.M. Said I
          was leaving the hotel. Desk clerk
warned me: "Other hotels are worse than the
one you're already in."

     Luncheon on the screened porch (Black
          Mountain). Lake and the Smokies beyond.
Student kept plaguing David Tudor with
     questions. "If you don't know, why do
          you ask?" Day after we got through
               Arizona, the road was closed. Food
was brought in by air to keep the
     Indians and cattle alive. Pillows and
     sheets and blankets. Put them on the
          floor. The bed is too soft. We had
     one performance: Notre Dame. We drove
          all the day from New York and then
     back. A prom had been scheduled the
same night. We had an audience of
     sixteen: six priests and ten nuns.

Kilina and Charlie helped prepare the
Berkeley dinner. Forty of us.
Spaghettini al pesto (to clean and chop the
basil took five hours), fried chicken,
and salad, and, for dessert, black or red
raspberries (or both) with ice
cream. Suddenly the car went full circle
on the ice: it came to a precariously
tilted stop ten feet down in a ditch.
A truck driver having all necessary
gear soon stopped and got us back on
the road. We asked how much we owed him.
"Nothing," he said. "It happened to
me once and they charged me an arm and a
leg."

Like Lenny, David Tudor didn't get a
sandwich at Joe's. He didn't buy
anything else there. When we were on
the road to Ithaca, I offered him some
of my sandwich but he didn't want it. I
asked him what he had with him to
eat. "One Jerusalem artichoke; one
red pepper; one flask 'medicine-man';
one papaya." I'd played the piano all
evening (no preparations in it).
People came backstage afterward to see
what objects I'd placed between the
strings. Beograd's Festival gave
Canfield first prize. Cologne ridiculed
Canfield. When Clive Barnes writes
about it, he goes berserk.
Englishwoman wrote: "*Canfield* was
marvelous: I didn't want it to stop
ever."

Sandra: rare roast beef, mustard on
rye. We spent the afternoon on the
lawns of Ricardo Gomis' estate
outside Barcelona. The tortillas were
delicious (omelets with potato and onion).
The weather was perfect. Even though we
were all there (*and* his five daughters and

many other guests) the space was such
it didn't seem like a large party. We
don't just get gas: we ask the station
attendant where the nearest best
restaurant is. Susanna ate her
smoked salmon and cream cheese. Then
she began thinking about chocolate.
We stopped for the night. Eau Claire,
Wisconsin. Asked the lady who ran the
motel where to eat. "Don't be put off by
the way it looks; go to the restaurant
in the gas station over there." Now,
whenever we're anywhere near, we make a
beeline for the traffic circle on the
west side of town, hoping the restaurant's
still in business.

We were invited to the Ribouds' in
Paris. They had just received a large
box full of fresh mangoes from India. We
kept on eating until they were finished.
In a Buffalo hotel Sandra and Jim stayed on
the eighth floor. They had a large can of
sardines for breakfast. Five they didn't
eat they flushed down the toilet.
After paying the bill at the desk, Sandra
went to the ladies' room. There in the
bowl of the toilet were two of her five
sardines. We stopped at a small
crowded restaurant on the road between
Delaware and Baltimore. After our orders
were taken, we waited a long time.
The waitress finally came with some of
our food. Hastily, she said to Carolyn,
"You're the fried chicken," and to
Viola, "And you're the stuffed shrimp."

Picnic preparation in hotel room.
Chicken, marinated in lemon and *sake*,
wrapped'n'foil, left overnight, next day
dipped in sesame oil and charcoal-broiled.
Broccoli, sliced, was put with ginger in
twenty-five packages; corn, still in

husks, silk removed,
buttered'n'wrapped. Noticing bathtub was
full of salad, David said, "I don't want any
hairs in my food." In addition to the
roast beef and cheese on rye, Robert had
triscuits, a sour orange from Jaffa, a
banana, and some apple pie. David's sticky
fermented Passion-fruit juice geysered on
the way to Grenoble. Bus floor and
handbags were cleaned and the windows
were opened. Then it geysered again.

Three kinds of potatoes (boiled,
French fried, pan fried); *schlagzahne*
(unsweet whipped cream with chocolate
sauce): that was the Holland Festival.
After Merce got the Guggenheim
Fellowship, someone asked him what he was
going to do with all that money.
Answer was monosyllabic: eat! Had picnic
on the lawn in front of Howard Johnson's.
Went in and used the toilets. Then
drove away. We were in a California
bungalow Japanese restaurant on the
Strip. The food was surprisingly
delicious. The waitress wore a
traditional Japanese costume. After the
meal she asked whether we wanted any
dessert. I said no, but changed my
mind: decided on pineapple ice. She
said, "Oh yes, that'll cut the grease in
your stomach."

There's no indication in any of his
writings that Thoreau ever ate a
mushroom. Asked the waitress in
Sacramento how the roads were to
Oregon. Said she'd had a letter
from her sister two weeks before saying
she was driving south, but she
hadn't seen hide or hair of her. We
parked the car and took the train.
Kamalini didn't eat. She stood

near the kitchen, examined each dish
         before permitting a servant to
pass. In four rows, sixty sat on pillows
   on the terrace. Woven leaf-cups, each
   with oil and wick, gave light. Each guest
   had a table, raised irregular slab
of grey-green stone, on it a rectangular
tray with bowl for each dish, leaf for
         the pickles and chutneys.

Turkey-and-ham sandwich on rye
         (tomatoes'n'lettuce); pickle; two
   bottles Kirin beer; four candy bars.
   Merce ate half of the sandwich on the
bus between Albany and Ithaca, the other
   half in the motel before dinner. It's
   April 7. Spring's two or three weeks
   early. *Helvella* was already seen in
Brockport! I saw hepatica and bloodroot
   in Ithaca! We're going to Athens in
         southern Ohio. Every mile (we're
         going 70!) brings us closer to
morels! During our world tour, dancer
   got married, left company; itinerary
   changed: Air France confiscated our
         tickets, demanded more money. Our new
air mileage was less than our purchased
         air mileage: we requested refunds.

   Kraps told me more'n'more people have
         small farms. There's a blurring
   of distinction between Amish, Jesus
   Freaks, university graduates.
         Exchanging food with one another,
         they make their own economy. "Don't
touch money," they say. "That way we'll
         be free of government." I
explained to the cook in the motel how to
   make the stuffing for the eleven
chickens: the giblets, celery, parsley,
onion, and mushrooms chopped and sautéed in
         a pound of butter and added with eggs
and walnuts to the seasoned crumbs with

salt, pepper, and sage. Later he asked
        whether he should cut the chickens
in half before roasting them.

Now that I'm getting older, I think I
        understand what Wittgenstein had on his
                mind. He said if he found anything
he could eat he would stick to it and not
        eat anything else. Don't worry about
                Chicago. Brunch at Carroll
                        Russell's. Omelets and salads
after the show at the Sagans'. Skip's
        home cooking. The French restaurant on
                the north side that doesn't have a
                liquor license but's next door to a
                wine shop. Berghof's in the Loop.
                        One way to tell how hard we're
working is whether we have time to eat
anything other than hamburgers. Just as
we were on our way down into the desert, I
        noticed a large stand of *Tricholoma
                personatum* underneath the pepper
trees. We stopped and we picked them.
                They were in perfect condition.

Birthday cake in Shiraz in Iran had an
                icing decorated with pomegranate
        seeds. We'd been on one train from
Warsaw to West Germany, our theater
        luggage on another which hadn't arrived.
        No way to get information from railway
                authorities in East Berlin. A day
                passed. Consulted *I Ching*. Oracle
                said: Don't worry, relax and feast.
                        While we were stuffing ourselves,
                news came that our trunks had just
                arrived. New farms in Appalachia.
Farmers take poor land and set to work to
        improve it. Kraps shares a farm with
                four friends. This year they're in
corn. Next year (they have deep loose
        soil) they'll get into potatoes and
grains.

We were waiting to be ferried
across the Mississippi. We had
nothing to eat. We waited two hours. It
was cold and muddy. When we decided to
leave, Rick and Remy had to push the bus
up the hill. Later we learned that the
ferry service had been discontinued two
years before. Jack Kiefer and Moss
Sweedler introduced me to the Moosewood
Restaurant in Ithaca. Luncheon.
Spinach and mushroom soup. Jack and
Moss had asparagus soufflé. I jumped to
dessert: yogurt cream cheese pie
(nuts in the crust). Milk that was
actually milk. Backstage: crew's playing
poker. Holiday Inn: Room 135. Four
cups of ground walnuts; 4 cups of
flour; 12 tablespoons of sugar; 2⅔
cups of butter; 4 teaspoons of
vanilla. Form into circa 125
small balls. Bake at 350°
in motel oven. Now back to Room 135.
Roll in 1 pound of powdered sugar.
Nut balls.

About 8:00 P.M. we arrived in Durango.
There were two or three
conventions. All the motels and hotels
were filled up. Drove up and down the
main street until we finally landed in
an old whorehouse. Each room had a bed
and that was all. No windows. No water.
Bathroom with toilet was down the
hall. Sign on Tennessee Thruway:
You've just passed the best fried
chicken in the world. We got off at the
next exit and drove back. Except for
Lois Long's fried chicken, it *was*
the best we'd ever had. There were
collard greens, black-eyed peas, okra.
You could eat as much as you wanted.

Asked Moosewood waitress how many

people and how many hours were
necessary to keep Moosewood going.
She said: "There are fifteen of us; we
choose our own hours." What about
shopping? "We do it by telephone."
Health food. Théâtre Experimentale.
Théâtre Gonflable (inflated rubber
theater at St. Paul de Vence). For
rehearsals during the day it was as
hot as an oven. For the evening
performances it was freezing cold.
There was no room for the musicians.
Sound was piped in from a truck
outside. Air France's so large it's
impossible to know what part of it to
talk to (even within our company
there's a certain lack of
communication).

Meg Harper had three apples and a
bottle of red wine. She bought a dill
pickle and several slices of roast beef.
When Merce was in residence at Illinois,
he stayed at the Johnstons', took all of
his meals with the family. Betty made
box lunches when he was too busy to return
home. Betty's cooking is delicious,
nutritious. For two years, I got
heavier and heavier. "When it comes
to desserts," Betty advises, "throw
health out the window." (Through
eating nothing but thistles, Mila Repa
took the form of a thistle. He was able
to transport himself wherever he
wished.) High above, thistle floated
past. One farmer to the other, "Pay no
attention: it's just Mila Repa."

Vitasok's thick fruit juices are
great. Had'em first in Zagreb, and
recently in Beograd. In Ljubljana's
supermarket, I bought twenty-four
bottles of raspberry. When we come into a

new town, David Tudor goes over the list
of restaurants in the Yellow Pages. "How
do you read it?" "I read the ones in
large type face first; depressed by
that I start from the top
regardless of type face and read all the
way down to the end." Julie read the
list of sandwiches in the delicatessen but
didn't buy one. She had just had a
cheese omelet for breakfast. After
six weeks in Japan, we went back to Stony
Point. How was Japan? "The pickles
were delicious."

We had stopped for gas in Ohio.
While the dancers were going to the
toilets, buying snacks, and doing their
exercises around the pumps, the station
attendant asked me if we were a group of
comedians. I said, "No. We're from New
York." Waiting for air tickets to
Prague. Outside his Albany room, on
the window ledge, Charlie had left some
apricot yoghurt and a package of
Swiss cheese. The sandwich he bought
at Joe's had three kinds of meat: bacon,
turkey, and chopped liver. Friends
in Gaudeamus wanted to take us to a
special restaurant in The Hague.
But we couldn't get in because of the way
I was dressed. The same thing
happened in Bremen. There,
however, Hans Otte persuaded the
manager of the restaurant to let us
sit down. But the people at the next
table immediately got up and left without
finishing their food.

I think it was Remy who got the idea to
advertise the company as America's
Best Fed Dance Company. That was in
pre–AGMA days when Merce paid for
all the food, gas, and motels, and

then gave each of us twenty-five
dollars for each performance. When
world tour was ancient history, Air France
gave a small refund on our tickets.
Valda was talking with the bus driver.
He seemed to be a family man, often
mentioned his wife and children. After
leaving us, he was going south; it
would be warm and beautiful. "Are you
going to take your wife?" "Would you
take a chicken salad sandwich to a
banquet?"

Jean's sandwich was turkey: white meat on
white bread, Russian dressing. In
retrospect the Ceylonese restaurant
in Boulder reminds me of Sri Lanka
in London. In each case the
cuisine was light and delightful,
and we were given a multiplicity of ways
to vary the taste of a dish.
Albert's luggage included many cartons.
Butane stove, basic utensils, staples
on hand. While we were reading menus,
he was cooking elaborate meals in
his room. Dancer on dressing room
floor, tormented, refusing to perform.
What'd she eaten? Driving along in
the late afternoon, we generally brighten
up: it is time for snacks and a drink.

Drought: found *tabescens* in Oklahoma City
park. They only had two kinds of bread:
white and rye. Chris chose rye (with
Virginia ham, sliced egg, tomato,
chicken salad, and mayonnaise). He drank
grape soda. Cunningham's breakfast: two
parts yeast, one part liver, one
part wheat germ, one part sunflower-
kernel meal, one part powdered milk (cold
pressed), pinch of kelp, one part lecithin,
one-half teaspoon powdered bone meal.
At home, mixed with milk and banana in a

blender. On tour USA, mixed with
milk in portable blender. On tour
elsewhere, mixed with yoghurt or
what-have-you. Sue Weil turns her home
into a hotel at the drop of a hat. I
always stay in the room opposite
Peggy's.

Dinners at Sri Lanka generally begin
with egg hoppers. An egg hopper is an
iddiapam made with rice flour and coconut
milk in the bottom of which fried egg
sunny-side-up is placed. On top of
the egg your choice of condiments from a
tray of many. EAT (Experiments in Art
and Technology): Merce never got involved
in it; David Tudor and I did. The
inefficiency of the engineers nearly
drove me crazy. They had no
realization of the truth of the fact
the show must go on. Began to give
Doolie the nut ball recipe. She said,
"Stop! I can't eat nuts. I have an
allergy."

Pontpoint: the company ate by
candlelight. Everywhere we've gone,
we've gone en masse. A borrowed
private car took two, two such cars took
six to eight, the Volkswagen bus
took nine. Now airplanes and chartered
buses take any number of us. Soon
(gas rationing) we'll travel like Thoreau
by staying where we are, each in his own
Concord: transmission of images, not
of bodies, television. Mila Repa. I did
most of the driving except in
emergencies. Going east from
Buffalo, we couldn't see a foot ahead
because of a blinding snow storm.
Merce took the wheel. Barbara found the
sandwich she'd chosen very good. Dressed
with lettuce, tomato, mayonnaise, and

mustard, and accompanied by half a dill
pickle, it was Swiss cheese and turkey on
rye.

After Jean'n'I'd rolled one hundred
balls, I remembered I'd forgotten
the vanilla. We started over.
Moosewood in Ithaca; Whole Earth
Restaurant in Santa Cruz. It's clear
what's happening: young people all over
America turning the country into a place
to be matriotic about. We reached the
western Pennsylvania park toward
midnight. Using flashlights, we carried
charcoal, food, and drink down the
path on the side of the cliff to the
grounds below where the fireplaces were.
May apples were blooming. Nick took
charge. We had drinks while the yams
were roasting. Mrs. Pylyshenko's stuffed
cabbage with mushroom cream sauce. Then
poker. That's how I met Fred Kraps,
Lighting Designer, Brockport's Dance
Department. Following day, Kraps
mentioned farm and counterculture while
we were eating Sicilian pizza.

Boos and bravos. Doug ate roast beef
on rye and drank Dorfmunder Action
beer. The simplest thing in the
technological world is amplification
by means of contact- and throat-
microphones. We arranged a banquet on
stage at the Y all the noises of which were
to go through a multichannel
sound system. EAT's engineers managed to
foul it up. Azuma (Japanese
restaurant in Ithaca). Excellent
tempura (not greasy; flaky, delicate
batter). I wrote to Black Mountain in
'39 asking for a job teaching music. No
reply. In '48 they said they'd put

us up if we'd perform there but that
they didn't have any money. We parked
the car and stayed three days.
While backing up to leave, we noticed
the space beneath the car had been filled
with presents.

"You go home now?" No; this ends the
first of five weeks. Toward the
end, Black Mountain didn't have a
cent. The cattle were killed and the
faculty were paid with beefsteaks. Chef
in Kansas motel-restaurant cooked
the mushrooms I'd collected. Enough
for an army. They came to the table
swimming in butter. Carolyn, who isn't
wild about wild mushrooms, had seconds. I
complimented the cook. How'd you know
how to cook'em? "We get them all
the time: I'm from Oklahoma." There's a
rumor Merce'll stop. Ten years ago, London
critic said he was too old. He himself
says he's just getting a running start.
Annalie Newman says he's like wine:
he improves with age.

The following text, finished in 1973, was first published in 1974 as an introduction to *The Drawings of Morris Graves*, a book edited by Ida E. Rubin for The Drawing Society, Inc. Its material derives from personal experience and recollections, conversation with the artist, one of his published remarks, and conversation with some of his friends, Dan Johnson and Marian Willard, Nancy Wilson Ross, Dorothy Norman, Xenia Cage, Merce Cunningham, and Alvin Friedman-Kein. Here and there I have introduced brief, unidentified quotations from *The Gospel of Sri Ramakrishna, Transformation Symbolism in the Mass* (C. G. Jung), the *I Ching* (Richard Wilhelm–Cary F. Baynes translation), Epiphanius, and Athenagoras as quoted by Hans Leisegang in *The Mystery of the Serpent*.

Series re Morris Graves

When I tried to imagine what it would be like to be Graves in the act of painting, it seemed to me it would be natural to vocalize and at times to dance. I then asked whether that happened. He said it did. For the nonsyntactical dance-chants, I used the syllables of names and words from *I Ching*–determined pages of *The Gospel of Sri Ramakrishna*. The arrangement of these syllables follows metrical patterns of the fourth movement of my *Quartet* for percussion (1935). It was following the third movement that Morris Graves said, "Jesus in the Everywhere." And it was the day after that event that we first met one another. After seeing Graves' series *The Purification of Cardinal Pacelli*, Xenia Cage and I arranged an exhibition of it at the Cornish School in Seattle (1937).

TA TA TA giTATAgiTATAgiTAgi
The brushes. Before I went to India, he
told me: Imagine that you're dreaming.
Land around the lake rests upon it obscuring
its shape, shape that needs to remain
unrevealed. Path returns upon itself. Leaving by
the front door, we go around the lake and come in through
the back. Leaving from the kitchen, after walking past the reeds
at the far end, we return as guests
invited to dinner. In a shop he noticed the sato
yellow plates (a yellow between custard and yolk of
boiled egg). And he bought the plates not
for himself but for an eggplant he did not yet
have so that, placed on one of the plates, the eggplant might be an
eggplant.

Fire over China. But when fire died
down, behold, only the Buddhist shrines had been destroyed.
All else O.K. Then southeast Asia and Tibet. Nothing
about India. Egypt a little.
Unexpectedly, Graves was prostrated, forehead on
floor, in the room in which
Ramakrishna had talked to the devotees.
Presence. maYAYAmaYAYAmaYAmaYAYAmaYAmamaYAYAmaYAmaYAYAmaYAYAYA
maYAmaYAYAmaYAma In the liturgy of Hippolytus the water chalice is
associated with the baptismal font, where the inner
man is renewed as well as the body.

Rolls Royce. Not just old: it was
vintage. It was elegant. It was the way for
those making revelations to be properly
transported. It was
necessary to leave the Rock. Navy air
training station had been established on Whidbey
Island. Flight pattern was out over Puget Sound and
then back over the Rock. Six, eight, or ten in
formation. The windows of the house would
quiver and rattle. garVIDyasaVIDyasaVIDyaVIDVIDyaVIDyagar
VIDVIDyaVIDyaVIDyasaVIDVIDyagarVIDyaVIDVID
ya No morning passes without his opening the
book. Day begins. There are
few markings. The paper pages have begun to feel like cloth. The
state of a servant's house will tell you clearly
whether his master has decided to visit. Purification. The
chalice is a fruit one half of which has
been removed. Old brushes
aren't thrown away. They become recognized in
detail. "O there you are." Escalator. Removed his shoes
and sent them up. He followed stockingfoot.
Choose any one that you want. Greedy friend took twelve.

Instruments for New Navigation. Constructions using
precious materials, marble, mica, bronze, Venetian
glass. To assemble them, he employed
Irish craftsmen. He was not satisfied
with their craftsmanship. Few have been shown.
JAI JAI maJAIJAImaJAIJAImaJAImaJAIJAImaJAI
mavaSISIvaSIvaSISIvaSISISIvaSI
vaSISIvaSIvaSISIvaSISIvaSISIvaSIvaSIJAImaJAImamaJAIma
JAIJAImaJAImaJAIJAI A discovery on a lost lake
shore which held, juxtaposed superbly, a need and its
fulfillment which had the intensity of a revelation. While it
occurred something was known anew
about where and how the best in life
transpires. Anacortes. We stood back from
the precipice. Beyond
it he danced on a ledge. Frightened he'd fall into the
valley below, we begged him, we shouted,
"Morris! Please! Come back! Come back!"
He didn't stop. Wild dance continued. The receptive brings
about sublime success,
furthering through the perseverance of
a mare. If the superior man undertakes
something and tries to lead, he goes astray; if he follows, he
finds guidance. Quiet perseverance brings good
fortune. Dive deep, O mind, dive deep in the Ocean. The
painting paints itself.
Child is born. Our activities are
peripheral (we make love; a pregnant mother follows a
certain regimen: asked to construct a
spine or brain or heart, she'd say, "I can't"). Third, the floors
are swept clean. Unless forced into the den,
he'll stay with the lions outside.

He'd been going through
my mind; then there he was as though
fulfilling an engagement. That seemed
strange. Philip told me it was even stranger: he'd not been
expected; he'd traveled more than two
hundred miles. Ireland was not noisy at
all. There were, of course, a few intercontinental flights,
but nothing serious. The problem was the Irish, the people
themselves.

Show me about America! The country appeared.
Striped vertical aurora (red-white-blue and red-white-blue) along the
eastern seaboard. The jewel. I have never
seen him with brush and paper (twice he's made pen
drawings when I was present: once at a
Christmas Eve party when presents were being
exchanged; once in a guest book). The
jungle around the house is cleared up. He had removed all the
seats and put in a table and chairs so that the
old Ford was like a small furnished room.
There were books, a vase with fresh flowers, and so
forth. Wound. Spastic, like madman in the
street. Friend walked up: stop it this minute!
Just stop! Spastic burst into tears, then roared with
laughter. "Thank you: no one speaks to me that
way." Identification. TRAI yaTRAILOKya Hers
is a female form. She is the Mother.

Spotted over the whole
country in five different places: great medallions of the
Founding Fathers. Washington appeared twice: in profile
wearing tricorn hat. Others had wigs.
Each time I touch you it is
you this same way. Dinner arranged so
two collectors who owned works could meet him. Wishing to leave the
party early, he used the excuse that they'd called him by
his first name.

They have a snake which they keep in a certain chest and which at the
hour of their mysteries they bring forth from its
cave. They heap loaves upon the table and summon the
serpent. Some of us are sentient, some are
non-sentient. All of us are beings. Once he drove
up to a luncheonette, parked, opened the door
on the curb side, carefully unrolled a red carpet across
the sidewalk. Then he walked on the carpet, went in,
and ordered a lettuce
sandwich. Meanwhile, a crowd
gathered. What next? How could you do this to
me? There must be certain stores where he buys
it. Or is that why he travels around the
world? The paper. He keeps it; and, once
prepared to set a sheet of it alive, examines each,
finding each remarkable. A party was arranged. The guests, mostly
museum officials, were chosen by him. They
arrived but he didn't. He sent a friend to say he wasn't coming.
dhiSAMAdhiSAMAdhiSAMAdhiMÁdhiSAMAdhiMAdhi
dhiSAMAdhiMAdhiSAMAdhiMADMAdhiMAdhi
"Floating world." *Sung.* Rain, curtain
of windswept lake's surface beyond: second view (there are others,
he tells me, one with mists rising). Yesterday,
stillness, reflections, expanding circles. A
western garden: water,
not sand; vegetation,
not stones. Thunder.

1939. Malcomb lived downstairs. Morris,
Xenia and I lived upstairs. Morris had the front room. Xenia and I
had three rooms: kitchen and living room halfway down the
hall; our bedroom was at the end of the
hall just opposite the bathroom. "What is your
favorite quote?" LI LA Temple of Kali: people frenzied.
Six feet four, mind a whirlwind, Graves raised
his arm, smashed his
offering, a tangerine, on the image.

Laing was telling about the people who had been
born again. As they were being
born they made strange sounds and moved in
strange ways. After rebirth they embraced one another and
were given new names. After World War II there was a
move on the part of many to suburbs. Woodway Park had a lot of
unsold land. It was subdivided. Suddenly all
around the Edmonds house there were the
noises of machines. He hadn't
told us, but we knew quite
well that when his door was shut we were not to disturb him. Everyone
expected something strange to happen. However, all that
Graves did was eat the sandwich and
pay his bill, get back in the car,
roll up the carpet and drive away. daSASAtchiDAnandaNANdaSASAtchida
NANdaSASAtchiDAnanDADAnanDASASAtchiSAtchiSASA The brush
is not an extension of his
hand or arm. (His hand is not that of a
painter: his fingers are not
exceptionally long.) The brush is itself a brush. It
is another member of the same family. Greenhouse off the
kitchen began falling apart. Irish
workmen (wanting two jobs instead of one)
had carefully put insufficient cement in the mortar. No sooner were
they up than walls began crumbling.

Served him roast lark.

It crawls upon the table and rolls in the loaves. They not only
                              break the bread in which the snake has
                    rolled and administer it to those present, but each
                    one kisses the snake on the mouth. They gave me the
            ivory necklace of skulls. After several years I sent it
back. It belongs, I said, in India. Now that India's here, I
                          want it back again. The lake is a cup
                              full to the brim. CHAI yaCHAI
        TANyaCHAITANyaCHAITANyaTANyaCHAITANyaTAN
        yayaCHAITANyaCHAIyaCHAITANyaCHAICHAITAN
        yaCHAIyaCHAITANyaCHAIyaCHAITANyaCHAICHAI
                              Finally, the master himself
                    sends various things to the house, such
            as a carpet, a hubble-bubble for smoking, and the like.
            Friedman-Kein saw thirty *Instruments for New
                    Navigation*, elements for forty more. Told Duncan
                          Phillips how marvelous they were. NASA
            invited Graves to Goddard Space Flight Center and Cape
            Kennedy to discuss aesthetics of orbital travel. Came
        to the concert with friends, a large bag of peanuts, and
                    lorgnette with doll's eyes suspended in it. "If
                    he does anything upsetting, take him out."
                          After the slow movement, he said:
        Jesus in the Everywhere. That was taken as the signal.

Family saga: the animal appears. And he? He
disappears: to reappear in it. So when you see these things
arriving, you conclude that the master will very soon
come.

It was not at night. It was during the day. A vision of
various civilizations. China.
Tibet. Egypt. America. India missing. Going to the outhouse
one went through thick weeds five feet high. Once
inside, the situation was reversed: outhouse was filled with weeds that
were hanging from the ceiling. The best thing to do
is to leave the audience and go up on the stage, and there, if the
spirit is not moving, to remain immobile.
There are times, however, when it is necessary to
leave the theater. KRISH KRISH naKRISHKRISHna
KRISHKRISHnaKRISHnaKRISHKRISHna
KRISHnanaKRISHKRISHnaKRISHnaKRISHKRISHnaKRISH
KRISHKRISHnaKRISHnaKRISH House in the
Himalayas. As they carried him down the aisle, his
face upward as though he were on a stretcher, he found himself
passing beneath her large
bosom (it was she who had given the order). She said, "I am Mrs.
Beck." Morris replied: Good evening, Mrs. Beck. He can paint on
any paper. One on fine
paper had been folded to fit into an airmail envelope. He went to
Japan to study the art of mounting paper. When all is
said, what remains to be said? "O lonely. O help me
across the stream." Long long
distance call. Mrs. Beck
followed Morris and the men carrying
him outside to the patio. The fast drumming had begun
and was audible through the closed doors. Morris, released,
began dancing. "His dance," Mrs. Beck
later reported, "was very sinuous." Bird's wings on
her head. The sacrificial bowl in
her hand. Having found him, she stayed with him until
he died. Suzuki.

Extraordinary show of Japanese treasures. State Governor was
coming to museum's opening. No artists had been invited.
Proverb: Round outside and square inside. RA
His painting is *its* personality.
Skibberean (the gentleman's house) seemed too large. So when he
ran across the cottage in County Waterford, he took it. It
was smaller and easier to maintain.
Dorothy had returned to America. Richard had left for
Norway. The Rock. Graves was painting. Sudden sharp
knock at the window. No one lived for miles around. Graves turned,
saw beyond the pane of glass a deformed,
twisted creature calling for his lost brothers. It was months before
he had brush in hand again. Sri Ramakrishna not only
lived as a man, a woman, a
monkey: he lived for six months as a plant, standing
on one leg in ecstasy. Dinner with the Duchess of Kent.

Only way to reach the beach is to go through
the area where the redwoods have
been cut down. Desolation. On the beach there's a herd of wild elk.

Museum opening. Anyone at all who had money to
speak of had been invited. No artists. A distant relative
having an entirely different background paid a
visit to the family when they were staying in
Ireland. Stayed awhile, then went away.
He registered as a conscientious objector.
Drafted anyway, he was put on a train going south. He escaped,
'phoned in. Was put in the army stockade. Laying the fires. Log
across front holds fire to the back. Brick wall
reflects the heat into the
room. Otherwise, heat of the fire
goes straight up the chimney.
Taking out the ashes. Taking out the ashes. Laying the fires.
Friends in front: footman and chauffeur.
And the artists in the back: Jan, Dale, Patricia,
and Morris. Rolls-Royce. Aren't you sorry that you're
not a human? Edith wagged her tail
(Aren't you sorry
you're not a dog?). Who are you? Why don't you speak? Why
do you do this to me? What do you want?
The house is a chalice that has a lid on it and it is not
round. The garden's not like the one
that surprised Edgar Anderson in Mexico: it's weeded, clearly
distinguished from lawn and terrace by low,
stone-grey masonry wall. KSHA KSHA KSHA raAKSHAraAKSHAra
KSHAraAKSHAraKSHAraKSHAAKSHAra
KSHAraAKSHAraKSHAAKSHAraKSHA
raAKSHAraKSHAraAKSHAraAKSHAraAKSHAra
KSHAraKSHAKSHAraKSHArararaKSHAraKSHA

"Revered sir, who is giving you milk?" "Brother, He
who beat me is now giving me
milk." Anything can happen. The reason's
this: any one or number of the elements can
remain as is; any one or any number of the elements can
change into the opposite. I must close the
door, for if I leave it open nothing will happen. He had time:
we never walked quickly; climbing was slow.
When we reached the turn in the stairway, he
was motionless, flat on his back, spread-eagled
head downward on the
steps, face streaked with dark red paint.
The scientists were pleased with Graves' proposal:
an amethyst on the end of a gold-plated boom. Talisman. Mexico,
Yucatán, the Caribbean, Venezuela and ten days in Rio,
Mauretania, Morocco. Loudspeaker (army prison
yard): "Graves! On the gate!" Sergeant
gave razor and brush and ten
minutes to shave his beard.
Graves didn't shave. Cursed and warned
him: "If in ten more minutes you're not shaved,
we'll force-shave you and your face'll be
like hamburger!" VA VA tiPANPANchaVAVA
tiVAtiPANPANchaVAti I said that music's
excitement takes place in public, that when a
painting's finished the artist sees it at once,
that celebration's reason enough for so
many artists turning alcoholic. He said
it would not appeal to him to have a drink
while working.

He arranged a sprinkling system: to enter the house
guests passed through water, lightly falling water, like light
spring rain. Seeing that he didn't want
the sheep to get into his garden, they cut a post of the gate
at ground level so that the sheep could easily
push it up and pass under.
"Sheep think better than we."

A house: private environment; proportion and
space. One should not reason too
much. You get clear water if you drink from the
surface of a pool. Plate.
TA TA TAgiTATA Shower's in the bathroom, not in a cubicle.
The opposite wall's a mirror. Steam
from the hot water produces the slow disappearance of one's image.
Pleasure of having a body. "Waiting for the gift from me to me of
death." 3:00 A.M. Irish tenor singing
loudly in our living room. Without knocking, having left
his bed, Graves entered, carrying wooden
birdcage, bottom of which
was missing, plopped it over the tenor's head, said nothing, left the
room. No further singing that
night.

Escape. Army command: Sweep the floor! He swept it
perfectly. Decision: he's not insane. You
couldn't move in the room except sideways and you had
to stoop. It was furnished with large tables, each with full
complement of chairs. Throughout the
room, heavy rocks, bound with wire, had
been suspended from hooks in the ceiling. It's said it was an
egg to begin with that got
bigger and bigger and by friction was burst into two.
The top part came to be the
Heaven; the lower became Earth. Aerial
relationship. Schlossberg: we are finding ways to transfer
energy by means of light, like the sun does,
rather than by exploding mass.
Sudden sense of identification, spirit
of comedy. He said that sometime after
we'd left, he and Ted Ballard got to
talking. Ted said, "The
difference between you and them is that they are looking for
solutions; you don't think there're any
problems." Your second favorite? The
Canadian Rockies. But not for a
house.

maSYASYAmaSYASYAmaSYAma

The heavy woven wire fence is high and strong. It
protects the garden from deer. You cannot
see it from the house. It is completely concealed in
the forest. Cattle in the drawing room when
first he saw the handsome eighteenth-century manor.
Bought it. Against their
inclinations plumbers installed
three bathrooms. After carpeting was down, water overflowed.
Plumbers had stuffed rags and rubble
into the drain pipes. Magician. La Conner house was
a theatre: twice a month a
complete change of program. NA draNARENdraNARENdraREN
draNARENdraRENdradraNARENdraNA Compost includes vegetable
refuse, autumn leaves, clippings, weedings from the garden. Soil and
compost-maker including bacteria are added. Wooden
enclosure is taken down each spring. Same
wood is used to build a new enclosure. When I paint, he
said, I paint standing up.

riHAHAriHAHAriHAriHAHAriHAriOM!HAHAriHAriHAHAriOM!HAHA
riHA Asked whether he did what I thought that he did, he said,
"Yes." He gave me an example. He
can imagine having a house
in Ceylon, the Tea Mountains. Old woman dressed
excessively: false eyelashes, high red hair, trinket
jewelry. (Others tittering.) Graves came near: You're
very beautiful. She smiled smile of light, "I thank you." Bird is a
chalice. Chalice is a bird. Chalice and
bird are breathing together.

His birds are not birds.
They are invitations to events at which we are
already present. Write it down: don't forget to reply. There are many
islands in the lake. No one of them is larger than a chair
or coffee table. They're covered with vegetation.
They are tree tops that have turned into receptacles.
Slippery clay-based soil. Eel River gravel was
brought to compact the road. Earth
takes five years to reach
the angle of repose. Each departure requires an
expense of energy. "Graves! Into
the Prison Office!" They had brought in the PX
barber. Beard cut short with
scissors. Then lather. Gentle shave. Like a cat
licking up thick cream. And have you heard
how he hit me with the loaf of bread?

He told me that weekend he would take the carpets to a stream in the
mountains. Stream would wash them. There was plenty of
water, and there were large flat rocks on which he'd
lay them out in the heat of the
sun. buRAMBAbuRAMBAbu The body's
a plate, as it were, containing the water of the mind,
intelligence, and ego. Brahman is like the
sun. It is reflected in
the water.

Mel begged to be allowed to shoot some wild ducks on the
lake. Since Morris was going
south for a week, he finally gave permission. "But only once
and never again!" After that, only the reckless
birds remained, and they at the far end of the
lake. His eyes had an indrawn look, like
that of a bird hatching her eggs. It may help if we try
seeing double or triple. Let's think that we're
entranced. Dinner: Washington, D.C.
Psychiatrist leaned forward. Stream of Freudian
questions. Graves finally put fork down, stood
up. "Enough!" To Alvin: "If you won't leave with me, I'll
find my way alone." They left. After these warnings,
signs of death will multiply, until, in
obedience to immutable laws, stark winter
with its ice is here. From gentleman's house to manor.
He lived in the house in FitzWilliam Square before
moving to Rathfarnman. FitzWilliam Square is
preserved by the Irish Georgian
Society. Front door: complex collage; photograph of a lamb
whispering into Pope Pius's ear;
mixed media. Sunset: Xochicalco. Goats.
Donkey in the great space in front of the pyramid. Wind came up as we
left. Circle with plus sign.
Plumed serpents. Next day
he put the circle with plus sign with his name in the guest book.
To do this he moved to another part
of the space. DE DE vaCHAITANyaCHAITANya
DEvaCHAITANyaDEvayaCHAITANyaDEvaCHAITANyaCHAITANDEyaDEvaCHAI
TANyaCHAI

Some works are warnings. He's not just prophet
of bliss: he's also a Jeremiah. How many *Snakes and Moons* were there?
He pointed out the ones that had something. He gave no
feeling that he planned to do anything about the ones
that were lacking. Last February, however, he
said, "I will give that a little more tension."
Harlem dormitory (Father Divine): private room
(skylight). yaSANKAraSANKAraCHARyaSANKAraCHARyaraSANKAraCHARyaSANKA
raCHARSANKAraCHARyaSANKAraCHARyaSANKAraSANKAraSANKAra
CHARyaCHARCHARyaCHARyayaCHARyaSANKAraCHAR
ya New Zealand's Milford Sound. Fine for a house
except for the people.

It is not always true that one decides to leave
where one has been. Sometimes one cannot resist going on to a
place where he has not yet lived.
His guests were not permitted in. But he'd arranged
matters so that they were able to
peek, to see that the party had already taken place.
West toward the sea, down the hill,
is a grove of alder. A road was made to get there with pickup truck.
Trees are cut down, sawed into fireplace
lengths, split into chunks. July to mid-October wood is
seasoned in the sun, then brought bone
dry into the shed. Passage from *The Gospel*: "I am
the machine, and Thou, O Lord, art the Operator. I
am the house and Thou art
the Indweller. I am the chariot and Thou
art the Driver. I move as Thou movest me; I speak
as Thou makest me speak." Where to
go? Twentieth century's everywhere. He sees
in the night: he listens.
He sees as blind men do. Aerial
relationship. Noticing each is free to move in his
own way ("the worship in his own way"). Breathing.
Luminousness. Iridescence. KES KES KES vaKESAvaKES I was
standing on Broadway when you could still go both
ways. He was sitting in the back of a taxi. The driver waited.
Graves wrote out a check and handed it to me. He knew
I had no money. I looked
at the check. I was amazed at his
generosity.

maRARAma Just as the brush cannot paint unless it is in his
hand, so hand needs brush to hold. I asked him whether he ever used his
fingers directly on the paper. "Now and then a thumb: just a
touch." They sold the gifts he gave them.

It was the bump in the road, the old car going over
it, that brought the puppies into the world. Jan in
sequins, 'twenties style. Earth's
condition is receptive devotion. The earth in its devotion
carries all things, good and evil, without exception. We need
the *Instruments for New Navigation*. They must all come
out of their wooden crates. There are
craftsmen here or if not here in some other country
who could put them together to his satisfaction. SA
SA vaSADHAnaSADHAnaSAvaSADHAnaSAvanaSADHAnaSAvaSADHAnaSASADHAnaSAvaSADHA
naSAvaSADHAnaSADHAnaSADHAnaSAva Work that could have been
done quickly was allowed to drag on and on. All
kinds of excuses were given. They
say one thing and do another. (Disgust.)
They're dishonest. Gaelic impurity: "There are
certain sacred parts of the body that are never to be
touched with water." He began to see
a lake, lake in his Eye's mind. The
search began. The color on the paper
when it was wet! Now it's dry. And then
again in Hong Kong: struck down. Invisible power.
What *Who*? Who *What*?

People and machines. Reduce or augment
their number of dimensions. That way's the way
to make them secrets.

The extension of pleasure through the house out to
house surroundings and, in an orderly way, into the day
itself. There are no engagements. (Preparation for
irresistible work.) Served him
roast lark. lahALALlahALALlahALLlahALALlahALLlahlahAL
ALlahALlahALAL The canyon is never without some movement of
the air. Its stream goes into the ocean. Its walls are covered
with maidenhair fern. Circumstances of the paper.
Circumstances of the mind.

Cuernavaca. Osmosis. The smoke moving in the air, for
instance. We both have beards, full
beards. I'm nearing the end. I felt dizzy earlier today.
What caused that dizziness? Dark element
opens when it moves and closes
when at rest. The time's dangerous. A man
ought to maintain reserve, be it in solitude or in
turmoil of the world. ram ram
ramBABAlaBABAlaBAlaBABAlaBAlaramBA
BAlaBAla He has refused. Perhaps he'll change
his mind. Invitation: to travel south to
make a series of lithographs. He was given a
pittance for the collection: one one-hundreth of its appraised
value. While you're in Gangtok, levitation, for one
thing, seems to be a
practical matter. (Mila Repa traveled in the air in the form of
thistledown.) This changed sense of what's reasonable
diminishes as you leave Gangtok. OAO:
Orbiting Astronomical
Observatory. Solar energy
absorbed by the glass-covered wings. After
their unfolding, a revolving telescopic
camera would come out to record the heavens.

He had bribed the guard so he might stay overnight in the
pyramid. He arrived at the dark appointment.
Then, recollecting having stretched out in the
sarcophagus, he changed his mind. Back to
Cairo quickly. daDAMNDAMNda He alone was served roast lark. Rock was
rock. No water on it. Every week
into Anacortes to get water at a gas station. Carried it in
eight twenty-five-gallon wooden kegs placed
in the back of the Model A
pickup. On the rough road coming home, water was
always lost. They fall down before it and call this the
eucharist, consummated by the beast rolling in the
loaves. Through it they send forth a
hymn to the Father on high. On his way to
Japan when he was in the army, Johns visited
the Art Museum in Seattle and was deeply
moved by a Graves he saw there: large bird turned toward a smaller bird
perched on its shoulder. Chain saws,
bulldozers, rototillers, powered lawn mowers. Then terrace
radios. Noise was unbearable. Three more: a yellow lower garment
brings supreme good fortune
(aristocratic reserve); dragons fight in the meadow,
their blood is black and yellow (inflation of
earth principle); lasting perseverance furthers (no advance, no
retrogression).

Change the shape of
technology. Shape it to allude to shape of a chalice. The amethyst
would be as large as a fifty-cent piece. On
the very end of a gold-plated arm fourteen inches in
advance of the body of the vessel itself. Talisman. Guide
asking permission. Receptacle. The house is a receptacle.
Each day begins the same way. Cup. Morning shawl.
The chair outdoors he sits in, facing the forest. The book. The bowl
of cereal. Morris,
immaculate, in tails wearing sneakers. Jan
in sequins, 'twenties style. naBRAHBRAHmaJNAJNAna
BRAHmaJNAJNAnaBRAHmanaJNAJNA

She could have helped him but wouldn't. A
few years later the skin cancer which had been removed from
his face appeared in the same place on hers. In one junk shop he
found the base of the shaving mirror, in
another ten miles away the rest of it and the
magnifying glass. You could tilt
it. There were further
postponements. "We must keep in touch." He returned
to Seattle. Received the letter. His plan had been
eliminated. No reason was
given. Letter: mysterious energy. Cable from
Dorothy Norman: Insufficient oxygen. You were very high. And
do you sing and dance? Not with words
but with the sounds that language had before it began?
He gave an example. Sometimes a word's included.

Chalices. Each of us having spinal trouble. We slept and sat on
boards. And laughter (next year we'll be in
wheelchairs). I was surprised when he told me that
he was considering letting any and all of the hippies
he'd met have land on the shore of the lake. "No one will throw
you out." SI SI jiSISIjiSISIjiSISIjiSIji
jiSISIjiSIjiSISIjiSISISIjiSIjiSISIjiSISIji
Which is the most offensive aspect of technology?
Its smell? The look of it? Its effect on food and water? Its
sounds? Or is it that anything anyone does with his hands seems
useless in the face of technology's lavalike
continuation? When the door was finally opened
there were drawings and paintings everywhere: on all the
furniture, including the bed; on the walls and the
ceiling. We had to walk carefully so as not to step
on them. The table had not been cleared. There
were scraps of food on the plates. Stem removed. An eyelike shape
remained. Bird waiting to be born. Deep in the Ocean. If you descend
to the uttermost depths, there you will find the gem of Love.
Go seek, O mind, go seek Vrindavan in your heart, where with His loving
devotees Sri Krishna sports eternally. Was Graves with us when the
earthquake took place? All the people who had
never met, even though they lived next
door to one another, met then and there in the vacant lot.
Conversed with one another.

Now there is no escape. Tanzania, Uganda, Egypt, the islands of
Greece and Greece itself, Italy, France, New York. The King of Sikkim,
Graves told me, has rare clarity of mind. He is a
devout Buddhist scholar. His
meditations are those of a guru. His
conversation's not chitchat. It conveys the best of
his mind. The more closely attention is given, the
more difficult it becomes to
fix something by name, or by relation to other
things. It begins to move on into
another being. Floor covered with sand. Large tree
trunk that'd drifted up on the beach off center in the room, ice
cream chairs in circle facing it. Cawing of the crows,
patiently trained, made
conversation impossible. They stayed where he'd placed
them: on top of the driftwood. Communion. The blood. He wasn't a
student. Why wouldn't they let him in the
school? giTATAgiTATAgiTAgiTATAgiTAgigiTA I suggested sitting
down. He said that way he'd have to have other brushes.

Unwashed dishes temporarily put out of sight in
drawer lined with silver paper.

He filled a baby carriage with rocks and,
with strings, made a trailer for it of
toothbrushes. He pushed it downtown to the Olympic
Hotel, through its halls to the
main dining room. After placing a rock at
each chair but one, he then sat down and
ordered dinner. Seattle. They enjoyed an
immediate friendship. They talked about the mystery of death, the
nature of the next
dimension. Before long a certain
lightheartedness entered into their conversation. He could not tell
whether he was awake or dreaming or whether what
was happening was happening. Titan missile had been getting bad
publicity (two launchings had gone sideways into the
ocean); Pentagon feared greater publicity would
affect NASA funding. NANG taNANGNANGtaNANGNANGta
NANGta Second, the soot and dirt are removed from the rooms. In
this totality the conscious mind is contained like a
smaller circle within a larger one.

Petroleum fire. USA: red-orange.
Canada: forest green. Ashes. Out of Gulf rose huge
Negresses moving like gorillas.

Has he told you anything about the actual
process of painting or drawing? "Work periods are often very
long, going through the night into the next day or days." He continues
until the spirit leaves. Portico over
the terrace was supported on one side by the house, on the other by
handsomely rough-sawed hexagonal tree trunks
used as columns. There was a pool with lotus. The school's registrar
was coming to lunch. Just
when she was to arrive, there was a knock at
the door. Xenia opened it.
Morris, stark naked, was standing in the hall.
Zosimos: "And everything will be moistened and
become desiccated again, and
everything puts forth blossoms and everything withers again in the bowl
of the altar . . . For nature applied to nature
transforms nature . . . all things hang together."
ra

They used rafts, piling on them duckweed and water strawberry that
had grown too thickly, moving slowly from bay to bay.
As they continued their work, more and more the sky and
the forest were reflected in the surface of the water.
Repeating what he had told was taken as an insult. He
threw the cup of boiling tea. I was obliged
to leave the room. The Duke and the Duchess.
Photographer looks at you but snaps
himself. Fisherman's transformed by what he
catches. Three tables? Or is one
sufficient? Providing it's large? The colors to the
left, the brushes to the right, the paper
directly in front. And the water? Surely it's here and there,
right and left, ready no matter what. Minnow
has put the egg back together again.
Amazonlike demonesses and nearly naked. They were replaced by
thousands of stick figures:
ants moving through the ashes.
RA maRARAmaRARAmaRAmaRARA
maRAmamaRARAmaRAmaRARAmaRARARAmaRARAmaRARAmaRARAmaRARAmaRARAmaRA
Surface of the water responds to the
currents of the air and to birds, their floating, their takeoffs,
their touchdowns. My work is done: now the telephone
comes off the hook. Time for a nap before supper.

The footman rolled out the red carpet up the
museum steps. liKAKAliYUYUgaKAliYUYUgaKAligaKA
KAliYUgaKAKAliKAYUKA We fly
to place where no airplane is.
Secluded house throbs with
utilities.

The wise man gladly leaves fame to others. He does
not seek to have credited to himself
things that stand accomplished, but hopes
to release active forces. He was offstage left, invisible to the
audience. After hearing his
wail, people were mystified.
They asked: How was that sound
produced? (Not who had sung it, but what strange instrument was it
that had been used?) Both sides of the windows
are washed. Windex spray and paper
toweling instead of soapy water and cloth. Variation is
introduced: some outside,
then some inside. How many
windows are there? One hundred and two.
Are you sure? Yes, I am sure. In the next box the
Princess Chichibu was sitting (Hirohito's sister).

A student needed money for trip with girl friend to Mexico.
Morris gave it; then asked the young man for help on four
weekends around the house.
Student agreed to come at 9:00. Arrived instead
at 3:00. Left at 5:00. "Nobody here wants
to work." As we went upstairs, I paused to admire
the charcoal walls, their sheen and texture. He agreed they were
beautiful. He said there had been a fire.
Except in his bedroom, all the walls upstairs
were black. For that reason he had the
house rent-free. Hong Kong. Day after receiving vision he heard
of the assassination of Martin Luther King.
Did both events happen at the same
time? A shallow window next to the bathroom ceiling
goes the lengths of two walls. It looks to the forest beyond
the garden and lawn. On its ledge are many more or less translucent
containers, empty and having different
colors. Floodlights. Guest list.
They reached the museum before the Governor did. I
stayed in the flower market. He went to look for
a shopping bag. I ate the
jacima with lime juice and chili pepper. The bag he had had to buy was
plastic. There weren't any others. kaLANLANkaLANLAN
kaLANkaLANLANkaLANkakaLANLANkaLANkaLANLANkaLANLAN
LANkaLANLANkaLANLANkaLANkaLANLANkaLANLANkaLANLANkaLAN
kaLANLANka

RA RA naRARAvaRARAvaVAnaRARAvaVAnana The world is of
the nature of magic. The magician is real but his
magic is unreal. He left Ireland, finished the
eight-foot wall around the house at Woodway Park, sold the house
and returned to Ireland. Nouveau riche: Letting
this wood rat in, you've devalued our estate
by thousands. Wife, however, invited Graves to dinner.
Tycoon's talk turned
toward view: artists are loafers. Graves countered: Look! All
you have and use (all of it!) was touched first by an
artist. Qualities of life he regards most highly: that
it flow, continuity; that there be concentration, no
interruptions; privacy, all
the way to secrecy; the mysteries of consciousness (he finds the ego
tedious), life as karma and maya. Helped by
a friend who stood watch, he borrowed the fowl
from the zoo. When we opened
the door, fowl flapped its way in.
Xenia was terrified. Algeria,
Tunisia, Kenya. I told him
what Fuller had told me. "No reason for
you to drink: you're already drunk." He
laughed in agreement.

Is it Brahman's breathing that produces
civilization's changes? Kaliyuga. Exhalation. Making
matters worse. When will
Brahman inhale?

This is His sport. You must have
observed that all
the trees in a garden are not of the same
kind. His brother Wallace, far away, dreamt Morris
needed help. Up at dawn, took boat, bus, hitchhiked. Arrived at
dusk. Ten minutes before,
great stone had slipped.
Morris's leg was pinned underneath it. Morris
couldn't move. It wasn't that way at all. The
house has never been cold and damp. He
exaggerates. He gets carried away. I
wouldn't even dream of picking up an axe and smashing a stove to
pieces. Nor would I throw myself on the
floor. Each stayed in a lonely place until he
learned an animal's song and dance.
La Conner singing re-enacted the
learning. It was a teaching.
When others learned the song, the singer began to dance.
On a shelf on one wall: pink satin slipper,
blade of wheat, and perhaps some other objects I don't
recall. On the opposite wall: a painting
duplicating the arrangement. I touched both
arrangements in order to know which one was not
three-dimensional. jaKAKAliKAKAliPUjaKAKAliPUjaliKA
KAliPUjaKAKAliKAPUKAliPUjaKAKAliPUjaKAKAliKA
KAliKAKAliPUjaKAKAliPUjaliKAli Taipei,
Hong Kong, Japan, Bali, Singapore,
Ceylon, India again (two months), again Nepal (two
weeks), ten days as guest
of the King and Queen of
Sikkim. After dinner one
evening the King granted
his request. He spoke about the *essential* yeti.

Lost in the forest, don't move around; stay in one place. That way
you will be at the center, and
the center will act as a magnet, a magnet for
those who are searching. The proverb, he said, was an ancient
Chinese proverb. Alan Watts hadn't
ever heard of it. The chaise longue upholstered
with beige linen was in the bathroom.
Lying on it wrapped in terry cloth taken from the heated towel rack, you
could look out the window to the mountain and harbor.
The carpeting, wall to wall, was grey. Nature
creates all beings without erring: this is its straightness. It is
calm and still: this its
foursquareness. It tolerates
all creatures equally: this its greatness.
Man achieves the height of wisdom when all that he
does is as self-evident as what nature
does.

BRAH BRAH maBRAHBRAHmaBRAHBRAHmaBRAHmaBRAHBRAHmaBRAHmama
BRAHBRAHmaBRAHmaBRAHBRAHmaBRAHBRAHBRAHmaBRAHmaBRAHBRAH
maBRAHmaBRAHBRAHmaBRAHBRAH And the way in
leads to the way out. Ezekiel 47:1: "...he
brought me again unto the door of the
house; and, behold, waters issued out
from under the threshold of the house eastward.... and the waters came
down from under the right side of
the house..." Kneeling beside the stream, she lowered her head
to drink. Had she used her hand or hands as a cup, she wouldn't
have been frightened by the snake that
appeared in the water to meet her. Wheel.
Pottery. M.C.'s poem: Hands   Birds
(page's space between). Suzuki:
Hands   Dirt.

maBRAHBRAHmaBRAHBRAHmaSAKtiBRAHBRAHmaSAK Twice we have
visited Fern Canyon. Earth above, earth below (K'un
K'un): nature in contrast to spirit, earth in contrast to
heaven, space as against time. Devotion. No
combat: completion. The coexistence
of the spiritual world and the world of the senses. We
listened to the traffic of the birds. A
highway. When the Baroness Mitsuko Araki was asked whom she
wanted to meet, she said, "I only want to meet
artists." He was so miserably treated he disembarked
at Cherbourg, and spent five weeks in Paris. When he
finally arrived at the castle in Chichester,
nothing but obstacles were placed in his path. The
dinner was the last straw.

As we were leaving the airport Morris
said: First thing's to take a row on the lake. I said, "What
for? Mushrooms don't grow on lakes." Years later, Ted's
voice came over the water: "Mushrooms!"
Paddling out we filled the canoe with *Pleuroti*.

We were in the flower
market (Cuernavaca). We had gone up and
down the aisles where the fruits and vegetables
are. He was carrying several that he had
bought and planned to paint. His eye
was caught by a large clay pot with a plant in
it.

"I'm the happiest person I know." (S. W.)

She does this
makes yoU
fEel

that as far as she's concerned What
you'rE up to
Is the most important thing
in the worLd

and She
withoUt
gEtting

in the Way.
shE spends
her tIme
cheerfuLly

Solving problems
Until
thEy all disappear.

a great Woman:
shE
brIghtens society
by making performing artists usefuL members of it.

When Charles Aitel, representing a group of Norman O. Brown's former students, sent me a form letter in 1977 asking me to contribute to a cento in Brown's honor, I was delighted. The moment I had the chance I got to work with pleasure. This text includes references to other friends. The automobile accident happened to Teeny Duchamp. She has had to learn to walk all over again. It was with Edith Speziali that *Pluteus cervinus* was found in Scarsdale. Richard Martin Jarrell (Tom Jarrell, a two-time draft card burner) gave me, by example, the courage to learn to make bread, and Shizuko Yamamoto changed my diet.

Sixty-One Mesostics Re and Not Re Norman O. Brown

there is no difference Between
              this paRking
                         zOne and any other. the entire city
              is a toWaway
              zoNe.

which would you rather Be,
                  an aRtist
                    Or
                    a Work of art?
        that came up at the discussioN.

                    discussiOn
        as a form of art.

              let Others have theirs
    (we have ours): pun.

breakfast: the mOrning
newspaper.

first oBjective:
scaRsdale.
mushrOoms
groW
oN

heathcOte
near palmer.

find sOmething
to think.

yOu
were carried away.

we doN't
knOw
ouR
dreaMs
Asleep:
awake we kNow them.

                                        Behind
                        the medical centeR
                                        On a pile of chips
                pluteus cervinus (dry) Was
                                fouNd in quantity.

            nO place to go
is everywhere.

            it was Never
                pOssible
                foR all of us
            to hunt Mushrooms together: even when you'n'i first met
stephen wAs already
                liviNg away from home.

                                                theN,
                                                thOugh
                                i didn't know wheRe was there
                        i drove straight towards theM.
                                        it wAs as though
                                we'd had aN appointment.

            it has Become
            a pleasuRe
                        tO go to japan
        by staying at home in neW york
                        makiNg nuka pickles.

                                                            nO
                                                parking.

                        nO
            aspirin.

                    tiBetan
                 baRley bread
            with rOasted
            sunfloWer seeds
            ("the oNly

         bread yOu need to know how to make, the greatest"):
tassajara bread book.

what does it meaN when we say
                 sOmeone's
a complicated peRson?
                 soMeone whose reply's
         unpredictAble
              horizoNtally and vertically?

                                       what happened (autOmobile accident)?
                                       you tried to climb a tree.

tO
walk. starting all over again.

Beth
will dRive.
i will gO on
With
our coNversation.

i Begin
ciRca
twenty-fOur hours ahead of time:
that Way
the hard crust is thiN and crunchy.

cOnversation
is the staff of life.

it was Because
of Repeated audible failures
tO begin and a visible uncertainty of balance
that you made me feel i Was
iN a theater.

yOu held on to the lectern
as though for dear life.

the oNly way
tO
conveRse with you
is to be in the saMe room
or in the sAme car
or oN the same path:

the telephOne
doesn't work.

your stutteriNg's a basket.
it allOws you
to gatheR together
More
ideAs
thaN

a sentence Ordinarily would be able
to hold.

agaiN it happens:
nO
diffeRence between relevance
and irrelevance: More'n'more
All
thiNgs go together.

the day was saved By
dReaming:
Once
i Was awake
there·was Nothing

But
poetRy.
cOver it
With a damp cloth
aNd leave it in an oven with the pilot light on.

at the Beginning
it sticks to eveRything and falls apart
but as yOu
Work with it
it takes shape aNd

Becomes elastic. we've always meant
to be healthy but the last time we thRee were
in a health fOod store together
We were tourists
lookiNg

for sNacks.
my shOpping list today:
bRown rice,
sesaMe seeds,
tsAmpa,
peaNuts.

your seNse
Of
theateR
caMe through even on the recording.
but still i would rAther
have actually beeN

iN the hall
sO i could have seen you
while you weRe speaking.
Mix the flours with the oils,
your pAlms together, right-left,
as though you are marchiNg.

this is the first summer i've decided tO stay
in the city.

Sixty-One Mesostics Re and Not Re Norman O. Brown : 129

there are never any proBlems about how to spend
ouR time.
each Of us
has his Work
which caN always

Be left unfinished in the case
of chess oR
mushrOoms or
Whatever.
there's Never so much time

But that
i look foRward
tO the next time
We meet.
wheN will that be?

yOu and beth live
over three thousand miles away.

no one knows how to converse But you. is it because you do
so much Reading?
dO you talk to yourself
While
you're writiNg?

aNd
nOw
i do exeRcises. they began
because of Muscle
spAsms
iN venezuela.

i cOuldn't walk: i was crawling
on the floor.

a year later the pain Behind my left eye began.
the doctoRs
cOuldn't explain it.
i Was
takiNg pills

One after another
just in order to sleep.

the fuN we have talking
is to nO avail.
we neveR
coMe
to the end of A subject.
somethiNg always remains

to Be said.
you must make otheR
peOple
feel the same Way: that thought goes
oN and on —

mOuntain,
tranquility at the base of the mountain.

— that nOthing
ever comes to an end.

you've Never
tOld me.
aRe you still their father
and beth their Mother?
or Are you just
their frieNds?

to Become
fRee:
nOt
to knoW
whether we kNow or not.

visioN: family.
nO
fatheR,
no Mother.
just All of us.
us childreN. together.

the wind is blOwing
backwards.

we are in danger Of becoming
undernietzscied.

i never met your mother, But
i Remember
yOu told me
she Was
a clairvoyaNt or a theosophist,

i doN't remember which. she grew up
in ireland and yOu
weRe born in vera cruz
(i think that's what you told Me):
your fAther was employed there
as as aN engineer. (isn't that the way it was?)

where was he bOrn? tell me (you've told me, i'm sure, but please,
please tell me over'n'over, please tell me again).

In 1939 I bought a copy of *Finnegans Wake* in a department store in Seattle, Washington. I had read the parts of *Work in Progress* as they appeared in *transition*. I used outloud to entertain friends with *The Ondt and the Gracehoper*. But even though I owned a copy, no matter where I lived, the *Wake* simply sat on a table or shelf unread. I was "too busy" writing music to read it.

In 1942 Janet Fairbanks asked me for a song. I browsed in the *Wake* looking for a lyrical passage. The one I chose begins page 556. I changed the paragraph so that it became two and read as follows:

"Night by silentsailing night, Isobel, wildwood's eyes and primarose hair, quietly, all the woods so wild, in mauves of moss and daphnedews, how all so still she lay, neath of

Writing for the Second Time through Finnegans Wake

the whitethorn, child of tree, like some losthappy leaf, like blowing flower stilled, as fain would she anon, for soon again 'twill be, win me, woo me, wed me, ah weary me! deeply, now evencalm lay sleeping;

"Night, Isobel, sister Isobel, Saintette Isobelle, Madame Isa Veuve La Belle."

The title I chose was one of Joyce's descriptions of her, *The Wonderful Widow of Eighteen Springs.*

I remember looking in later years several times for other lyrical passages in the *Wake*. But I never settled on one as the text for another song.

In the middle 'sixties Marshall McLuhan suggested that I make a musical work based on the *Wake*'s Ten Thunderclaps. He said that the Thunderclaps were, in fact, a history of technology. This led me to think of Jasper Johns' *Painted Bronze* (the cans of ale) and to imagine a concert for string orchestra and voices, with the addition towards the end of wind instruments. The orchestra would play notes traced from star maps (*Atlas Borealis*) but due to contact microphones and suitable circuitry the tones would sound like rain falling, at first, say, on water, then on earth, then wood, clay, metal, cement, etc., finally not falling, just being in the air, our present circumstance. The chorus meanwhile would sing the Thunderclaps, which would then be electronically transformed to fill up the sound envelopes of an actual thunderstorm. I had planned to do this with Lejaren Hiller at the University of Illinois 1968–9, but *HPSCHD* took two years rather than one to make and produce.

Due to N. O. Brown's remark that syntax is the arrangement of the army, and Thoreau's that when he heard a sentence he heard feet marching, I became devoted to nonsyntactical "demilitarized" language. I spent well over a year writing *Empty Words,* a transition from a language without sentences (having only phrases, words, syllables, and letters) to a "language" having only letters and silence (music). This led me to want to learn something about the ancient Chinese language and to read *Finnegans Wake*. But when in this spirit I picked up the book, Joyce seemed to me to have kept the old structures ("sintalks") in which he put the new words he had made.

It was when I was in this frame of mind that Elliott Anderson, editor of *TriQuarterly*, wrote asking me to write something (anything, text or music) for an issue of the magazine to be devoted to the *Wake* (In the wake of the *Wake*). I said I was too busy. I was. I was writing *Renga* and had not yet started *Apartment House 1776* the performance date of which had already been set. Anderson replied that his deadline could be changed. I refused again and again. He persisted.

Anderson was not the first person to bother me by asking me to do something when I was busy doing something else. We continually bother one another with birthdays, deadlines, celebrations, blurbs, fund raising, requests for information, interviews, letters of introduction, letters of recommendation. To turn irritation into pleasure I've made the practice, for more than ten years now, of writing mesostics (not acrostics: row down the middle, not down the edge). What makes a mesostic as far as I'm concerned is that the first letter of a word or name is on the first line and following it on the first line the second letter of the word or name is *not* to be found. (The second letter is on the second line.) When, for instance, we were in a bus in Northern Michigan on our way to hunt morels (Interlochen music students were asking me what a mesostic was), I wrote

"Music . . .

(the M without an O after it)

"Music
  cOnducted . . .

(the O without an R) (the word "performed" would not have worked)

"Music
  cOnducted
   in spRing . . .

(the R without an E)

". . . by trEes: . . .

(the E without an L)

". . . dutch eLm disease."

To bring my correspondence with Elliott Anderson to a temporary halt, I opened *Finnegans Wake* at random (page 356). I began looking for a J without an A. And then for the next A without an M. Etcetera. I continued finding Joyce and James to the end of the chapter. I wrote twenty-three mesostics in all.

I then started near the end of the book (I couldn't wait) for I knew how seductive the last pages of *Finnegan* are.

my lips went livid for from the Joy
     of feAr
       like alMost now. how? how you said
   how you'd givE me
    the keyS of me heart.

        Just a whisk brisk sly spry spink
   spank sprint Of a thing
      i pitY your oldself i was used to,
    a Cloud.
   in pEace

Having found these, I looked for those at the beginning and, finally, as Joyce had done, I began at the end and continued with the beginning:

Just
A
May i
bE wrong!
for She'll be sweet for you as i was sweet when i came
down out of me mother.

Jhem
Or shen [brewed by arclight]
and rorY end
through all Christian
minstrElsy.

The bracketed words are the ones I'd have omitted if it were just now I had written them. There were choices to be made, decisions as to which words were to be kept, which omitted. It was a discipline similar to that of counterpoint in music with a cantus firmus. My tendency was towards more omission rather than less.

Just a whisk brisk sly spry spink . . .

became

Just a whisk
Of
pitY
a Cloud
in pEace and silence.

And a further omission was suggested by Norman O. Brown, that of punctuation, a suggestion I quickly acted on. Subsequently, the omitted marks were kept, not in the mesostics but on the pages where they originally appeared, the marks disposed in the space and those other than periods given an orientation by means of *I Ching* chance operations. Where, in all this work, Joyce used italics, so have I. My marginal figures are source pages of the Viking Press edition of *Finnegan.*

 Stuck in the *Wake*. I couldn't get out. I was full of curiosity about all of it. I read *A Skeleton Key*. . . . Ihab Hassan gave me his book, *Paracriticisms*, and two others: Adaline Glasheen's *a second census of finnegans wake* and Clive Hart's *Structure and Motif* . . . . I continued to read and write my way through all of *Finnegans Wake.*

 Finnegans Wake has six hundred twenty-five pages. Once finished, my *Writing Through Finnegans Wake* had one hundred fifteen pages. My editor at Wesleyan University Press, J. R. de la Torre Bueno, finding it too long, suggested that I shorten it. Instead of doing that, I wrote a new series of mesostics, *Writing for the Second Time Through Finnegans Wake*, in which I did not permit the reappearance of a syllable for a given letter of the name. I distinguished between the two J's and the two E's. The syllable "just" could be used twice, once for the J of James and once for the J of Joyce, since it has neither A nor O after the J. But it could not be used again. To keep from repeating syllables, I kept a card index of the ones I had already used. As I guessed, this restriction made a text considerably shorter, forty pages in all.

My work was only sometimes that of identifying, as Duchamp had, found objects. The text for *TriQuarterly* is *7 out of 23.* Seven mesostics were straight quotations, e.g., this one from page 383:

> he Just slumped to throne
> so sAiled the stout ship *nansy hans.*
> froM liff away.
> for nattEnlaender.
> aS who has come returns.

In such a case my work was merely to show, by giving it a five-line structure, the relation of Joyce's text to his name, a relationship that was surely in these instances not in his mind, though at many points, as Adaline Glasheen cheerfully lists, his name was in his mind, alone or in combination with another name, for example, "poorjoist" (page 113), and "joysis crisis" (page 395).

When I was composing my *Sonatas and Interludes,* which I did at the piano, friends used to want to know what familiar tunes, *God Save the King* for instance, would sound like due to the preparations between the strings. I found their curiosity offensive, and similarly from time to time in the course of this work I've had my doubts about the validity of finding in *Finnegans Wake* these mesostics on his name which James Joyce didn't put there. However I just went straight on, A after J, E after M, J after S, Y after O, E after C. I read each passage at least three times and once or twice upside down. (Hazel Dreis, who taught us English binding, used to tell us how she proofread the *Leaves of Grass,* an edition of which she bound for San Francisco's Grabhorn Press: upside down and backwards. When you don't know what you're doing, you do your work very well.) J's can thus be spotted by their dots and by their dipping below the line which i's don't do. Difficult letters to catch are the commonest ones, the vowels. And the consonants escape our notice in empty words, words the mind skips over. I am native to detailed attention, though I often make mistakes: I was born early in September. But I found myself from time to time bursting into laughter (this, not when the *Wake* was upside down). The play of sex and church and food and drink in an all time all space world turned family was not only regaling: it Joyced me (in places, that is, where Thoreau hadn't, couldn't, where, left to myself, I wouldn't've). I don't know whom to connect with Joyce ("We connect Satie with Thoreau"). Duchamp stands, I'd say, somewhere between. He is, like Joyce, alone. They *are* connected. For that and many other reasons. But that's something else to do.

I am grateful to Elliott Anderson for his persistence, and to the Trustees of the James Joyce Estate for permitting the publication of this work.

JOHN CAGE
New York City, May 1977

I

wroth with twone nathandJoe   3
                    A
                  Malt
                  jhEm
                   Shen

               pftJschute
               sOlid man
that the humptYhillhead of humself
      is at the knoCk out
         in thE park

                 Jiccup   4
              the fAther
                  Most
                hEaven
                 Skysign

                Judges
                   Or
        deuteronomY
               watsCh
               futurE

          pentschanJeuchy
                 chAp
                Mighty
               cEment
        and edificeS

            the Jebel and the   5
             crOpherb
              flYday
        and she allCasually
           ansars hElpers

                              Jollybrool
                              And
6   strupithuMp
                        and all thE uproor
                        aufroofS

                              to fJell
                        his baywinds' Oboboes
7   all the livvYlong
                              triCky
                              trochEes

              whase on the Joint
                        whAse
                        foaMous
                        oldE
                              aS you

                              Jamey
8   Our
                        countrY
                        is a ffrinCh
                           soracEr this is

        the grand mons inJun this is
                        the Alps hooping to sheltershock
              the three lipoleuMs this is
                           thEir
                        legahornS

                              Jinnies
                        is a cOoin her
9   phillippY
                        dispatCh
                        to irrigatE the willingdone

                              the Jinnies
                        fontAnnoy
                   bode belchuM
                        bonnEt
                        to buSby

10   this is the hinndoo waxing ranJymad
                           fOr
                   the hinndoo seeboY
                              Cry
                   to the willingdonE
138 : E M P T Y W O R D S

                     Jist   11
                   Appear
        toonigh Militopucos and toomourn
                   wE
                   wiSh for a muddy

                   muJikal   13
                   chOcolat box
                   i saY
                    inCabus
                   usEd we

       mammon luJius
             grAnd
        historioriuM
             wrotE near
             blueSt

                   Jerrybuilding   15
                   tO the
                     Year year and laughtears
                   Confusium
             hold thEm

      this carl on the kopJe
                   pArth a lone
       forshapen his pigMaid
                   hoagshEad
                   Shroonk his plodsfoot

             'tis a Jute   16
                 swOp hats and excheck a few strong verbs
                   Yapyazzard abast
      mutt has has at hasatenCy
                   i trumplE from rath in mine mines

             Jute
      one eyegoneblAck
      cross your qualM
             havE
             Sylvan

             obJects
             Olives beets
      oldwolldY
             Cargon of
      prohibitivE pomefructs

                              doublends Jinied
                                    mAy
                                    Mud
                                  sundEr
                          who oped it cloSeth

                                and Jarl   )
                              van hOother
                                  laYing
                                  Cold hands
                              on himsElf

                      and his two little Jiminies cousins of
                                  cAstle
                              be derMot
                                comE to the keep of
                              a roSy

                                  Jiminy
                              with sOft
                                  Years' walk
                              to tauCh him
                              his ticklEs

                      you were the doubleJoynted
                                  jAnitor
                              the Morning
                                    thEy were delivered and you'll be a grandfer
                      when the ritehand Seizes what the lovearm knows

                              hetty Jane's a child
                              she'll be cOming
                                  theY're
                                  tourCh
                              to rEkindle the flame

                              she'll do no Jugglywuggly
                              with her wAr souvenir
                                  Murial
                              assurE
                                  a Sure there

Jubilee   31
scAtterguns
faMily symbolising puritas
pEr
uSuals

Japijap
amOng
sibYlline
mulaChy   32
kingablE khan

practical Jokepiece   33
cecelticocommediAnt
his house about hiM with
invariablE
broadStretched

Juke and kellikek families
at One time
annoYing
C.
Earwicker

Jesses   34
ripe occAsion
our kadeM
villaplEach vollapluck
fikup for fleSh nelly

guinness thaw tool in Jew me dinner   35
Ouzel fin
a nice how-do-You-do
in poolblaCk
timE

Jurgensen's
shrApnel
coMmunionism
usucapturE
the Same

tongue and commutative Justice that there is   36
nOt one tittle of
hYpertituitary   37
mannleiCh
cavErn ethics

39   blue ruin and creeping Jenny
                eglAndine's choicest herbage
40   Man's
                     swEll
               that aimSwell

41   ì many Jiffies
        furbishing pOtlids doorbrasses scholars' applecheeks and
               linkboY's metals
                  Cross
               Ebblinn's chilled hamlet

                  subJects
              of king sAint
                 salMon
                  alivE
        with their priggiSh mouths all open   (

       a house of call at cuJas place
               Old sots' hole
                  bY
        setting a matCh to
               stEwards peut-être

42   Joined
              hAdbeen variety
            had stiMulants
          in the shapE of gee
             and geeS

43   Juiced after taking their
          liquOr from
        highwaY and brown byway
             sCotia picta
        and hE who denays it may his hairs be rubbed

           his maJesty
             thAt onecrooned king
             aMong
         rapsods pipEd
          decentSoort

45   Jail
             chOrus
      jail of mountjoY jail him and joy he was
             siCk
             sEven dry sundays a week

                    Joulting   47
                  the bAcktrap
                    oMnibus
               caught his dEath
                  of fuSiliers

                        (

                  mr J. f. jones   48
             colemAn of lucan taking four parts
               in *fenn Mac call and*
                    sErven
                    feerieS

                    Juxta-   51
             explanatiOn was put in loo of
                     eYes
                lokil Calour and lucal odour
                  to havE

          to sillonise his Jouejous the ghost   56
                of resignAtion
                    May gloat
                    Effective
                beam of Sunshine

                  kitnabudJa
                    tOwn
        or panbpanungopovengreskeY
                    their Compass   57
                      mElos yields the mode

            pro tried with Jedburgh justice
                    Acquitted con-
                    testiMony   58
                with bEnefit of clergy
                madthing haS done him

                    Judgements
                    thOse as
                    daYs
                      Camps
                    concurrEd

61
           Jilke
         begAn to
          Moult
       instEnch of
     gladSome rags

62
        poor Jink
         fOllowing
          roY's
63
        suCh bash in patch's
       bEyond recognition

−64
came down with homp shtemp and Jumphet
      to the tiltyArd
        froM
        a'slEep
ohny overclotheS

        reJaneyjailey
      walters Off
       whYte
      a pinCh
       idEal

leave astrelea for the astrollaJerries
  for the love of the sAunces
  puddywhackback to paMintul and roll away
      rEel
  and call all your Smokeblushes

65
      by a large Jugful
       sOmeplace
   on the slY where furphy he isn't by old grum
       Could
   canoodlE the two chivee chivoo all three

67
carcasses mattonchepps and meatJutes
    on behAlf of
 otto sands and eastMan
     wEnt and with
  unmitigated aStonissment hickicked at

68
      her Jambs
     each Other
   the nautchY girly
rapidly took to neCking
        sElling her spare favours

for the reJoicement of foinne loidies ind   71
    contrAstations
with inkerMann and so on and sononward
    flEe
    celeStials one clean turv

his manJester's   73
    vOice
had to fall theY
    slouCh
backwords *Et cur heli*

ziJnzijn zijnzijn   75
    hAsten selves
in a finglas Mill
    prayEd
on anxiouS seat kunt ye neat gift

    two Jars   82
and several bOttles though
    Ye
asked in the vermiCular
    with a vEry oggly chew-chin-grin

    Joking
    chAnge
    excelcisM
    rathEr
    amuSedly replied

    J. j. and s.   83
    befOre
firšt wind of gaY gay and whiskwigs
    wiCk's
    Ears pricked up

liberties of the pacific subJect   85
    circulAting
    seMitary thrufahrts
    opEn to buggy and bike
or quaker'S quacknostrum

Writing for the Second Time through Finnegans Wake : 145

86

the whole padderJagmartin tripiezite
cOpperas had fallen off him
quatz unaccountablY
like the Chrystalisations of alum
on Even while he was trying for to stick fire to

christies and Jew's i
bAllybricken
aniMal's sty
strEet
Sta troia

88

some maJar
bOre
erchenwYne
Crumwall
maximus Esme

89

tongue in a pounderin Jowl
mAthers of prenanciation
quare hircuM
no answEr *unde gentium fe...*
Siar i am deed

90

Jah and
i shOuld
Yes your brother
struCk him
bank in multifarnham whEther he fell in with

punic Judgeship
penAl law
91
stucckoMuck
had bEen removed
at the requeSt of

the gentlemen in Jury's
whO had been
those Yarns yearning for that good one about
Coddling doom as
stEak

92

pegger's windup cumJustled
neAtly with
the syMphysis of
antipathiEs
diStinctly different

festives and highaJinks and 94
nOw
a tradewinds daY and the o'moyly 95
rossies Chaffing
him bluchfacE and playing him pranks

and Jonnies
hold hArd
i'M glad a gull
for his pawsdEen fiunn
Sez he lankyshied gobugga ye sez

Jackass 96
the rOse
rogues lean to rhYme
there was never a marCus at all
among the marKEs

across the Juletide's 97
geniAl corsslands of
Mullinahob
bEaring right upon
tankardStown

the Jenny
hOux
and Yew 98
evereaChbird −99
glEam

Jest
gregArious
fieldMarshal
princE
myleS the slasher in his person

spike of smoke's Jutstiff 100
frOm
porphYroid buttertower and then thirsty
baCkwords
morE strictly

van diJke
grAvitational pull
chancedrifting through our systeM
quick spEak
dumb huSh

Jeer
tOo and
zhanYzhonies
and murrmurr of all the maCkavicks
shE who had given his eye for her bed and a tooth

Journey to
Ark see
the cooMbing of
the parlourmaids of aEgypt
placeat veStrae

he's my o'Jerusalem and i'm his
pO
my juckeY
from viCtrolia
nuancEe to

Jumbo
to jAlice
two ways of opening the Mouth i
not stoppEd
water where it Should flow and i know

the first book of Jealesies
childsize herOes
howke cotchme eYe
abe to sare stood iCyk
nEuter till brahm taulked him common sex

a Jolting
preArranged

Mountback against a partywall
bElow
uSe of quill or style

Jully glad
when christmas cOmes

aYe to aye
notiCing that
linEs

                    Jew   116
                    fAr
            in duMbil's fair
                    Ere
            our coaSts

        your maJesty
                bOost from
                allvoYous
                volapuCky
                gromwElled

            three Jeers   117
        for the grApe vine and brew
                ,ruM
                smElt
                    hiS end for him and he dined

            deJectedly   .   121
    in the diapered windOw margin
        basque of baYleaves all aflutter
                Curious
            protoparEnt's *ipsissima verba*

                    Jims
                    sAhib
        pipless as threadworMs
                innocEnt
            exhibitioniSm,

        quatrain of rubyJets   122
                withOut
                    loYal
            lobster loCks
                    you'rE another he hasn't

                    fJorgn   124
                    wAs
                he reMains
            postscrapt sEe
                    Spoils

                    looJing   125
                    tOrba's nicelookers of
                olderlY's
                    noClass billiardhalls with an
        had somE little laughings and some less of cheeks

126   Jhon
                                rAted
                               Mic
                               hE
               miSunderstrook and aim for am ollo

134   his indian name is hapapoosiesobJibway and his number
                   the plOugh took
         moves in vicous cicles Yet remews the same
          portobello equadoCta
                 thErecocta percorello

136   geulant on a fJeld duiv
                   ruz the hAlo off his varlet
       put a roof on the lodge for hyMn and a coq in his pot pro homo
                   thEn
           pancircenSor then hortifex magnus

138   màde man with Juts that jerk and
                   cOme whome sweetwhome
                shampaYing down
                  to Clouts
                and pottlEd porter

142   simon Jorn
                   bArty
                    Mor and tom
        and how war yorE
                maggieS answer they war loving they love

143   horsa's nose and Jeff's
                   gOt the signs of ham round his mouth
                violet's dYed
         what' sour lovemutCh
                but a brEf burning till shee that drawes dothe smoake

144   like Jolio
                   i hAven't fell so turkish for ages
           end of the Moon
           fool bought cabbagE head
                   i Shall answer to gracious heaven

145   the Jumps
                in her stOmewhere
                   maY they fire her for a barren ewe so she says
                   Cat you
                   mEek my

hairmeJig   146
   lAughing
   My
   risE out
   leaSt

    Jess katty   147
    lOu
   opsY poll queeniee ruth
in for the Church
     wE've all comefeast like the groupsuppers

 are you enJoying this
   breAk   148
   i aM
   i swEar i am
do you prefer itS in these dark nets if why may ask

 as none of yŏu knows Javanese   152
   minOr
   take Your head out of your
    faCts
    gripEs

  cheek by Jowel   153
with his frishermAn's blague
  for an aniMal   154
   ruralE
   abaSe you baldyqueens gather behind me satraps

  kelkefoJe funcktas   160
 · kelkefOje
   crYing to
   reCoil
 with a grEat leisure

 that is where the Juke comes in   162
   hAving
   chaMp̈aign
flop as a plankriEg
the twinfreer typeS are billed to make their reupprearance

 a king off duty and a Jaw
   gOod
somun in the salm *butYrum et mel*   163
   ut sCiat
   rEprobare malum et eligere bonum

recommending the silkebJorg
                    mAchine for the
              econoMical
              spacE to look
         mySelf a little more closely

168   would meself and mac Jeffet
                    fOur-in-hand foot him out
                    aY were he my own breastbrother
         bum and dingo jaCk by churl
         though it brokE my heart to pray it

                    i

169   Jem is
                         jAcob
         he was of respectable steMming
                    an outlEx
              between the lineS of

170   Juicejelly legs
                         mOlten mutton
171   greekenhearted Yude
                    attouCh
              what happEns when

172   Johns is
                    next plAce
              feel his laMbs
                         fEel
              how Sheap exex his liver

173   three Jeers
                    his rOtten little
         bottom sawYer till nowan
                    laCk
                    sEmantics

175   *sachsen and Judder*
               word mAde warre
                   heMpal
              must tumpEl
            broken eggS will poursuive bitten apples

                              american Jump   176
                                   fOx
                        are we fairlYs represented
                           in dreamColohour
                             battlE of waterloo

                            mothelup Joss   177
                         trousers chAnging colour
                                in cheMs
                                  rEvolted
                                  Stellas

                              in Junk et sampam   178
                                  On his
                                straY whizzer
                          to avenge maC-
                              jobbEr went stonestepping with

                          dr. poindeJenk   179
                              Authorised bowdler and censor
                            velluM
                            blundEred
                            an aiSling vision more gorgeous than the one before

                            the Jigjagged page   180
                              his tOngue
                          in his belfrY
                it took him a month to steal a marCh
                                hardsEt to mumorise more than a word a week

                              Jymes wishes   181
                              to heAr
                              druMcondriac
                                natE
                            really waS who

                          them bearded Jezabelles   192
                                  rOb
                              marYlebone
                while whistlewhirling your Crazy
                                  Elegies

                              all Jokes   193
                        go green in the gAzer
                                    Mr
                                  lEarn
                              to Say nay

black mass of Jigs and jimjams haunted by
innOcence
Yield our spiritus to the wind
pole the spaniel paCk
and thEir quarry

194 appears to the left at top.

,

'

198

iJypt
sAw *i*
lord saloMon
hEr
bullS they were ruhring surfed with spree

200
in a period gōwn of changeable Jade
that wOuld robe the wood
off her nose *vuggYbarney*
hello duCky
plEase don't die

202
tapting a flank and tipting a Jutty
pAlling in and pietaring out
¿   when Maids
wEre in arc
or when three Stood hosting

204
and me to do the greasy Jub   ¿
veřOnica's wipers
theY've moist
Crampton lawn
baptistE me father for she has sinned

205
or Jude's hotel
from nAnnywater
to the lootin quarter you found his ikoM
tipsidE down
cornerboyS cammocking his guy

the peihos piped und ubanJees twanged
with Oddfellow's triple tiara
206
she swore on croststYx nyne wyndabouts she's be
quiCk and
maguE

herself tidal to Join
    in the mAscarete o gig goggle
it's too screaMing
    minnEha minnehi
you muSt you must really make my hear it gurgle

    Jellybelly
incense anguille brOnze   207
describe her hustle along whY
    Can't you spitz on
whilE it's hot

shins between them for isabel Jezebel and   210
llewelyn mmArriage
a nightMarching
harE
and gumbootS each for bully hayes and hurricane hartigan

    a Jauntingcar
    dOolin
    coYle
a hairClip and clackdish
for pEnceless

    Jill the spoon   211
for jAck the broth
for Maggi
frozEnmeat
woman from luSk to livienbad for

    Jane in decline   214
sOaking and bleaching
the laundrYman
Cuffs was
hEir to the town

tell me of John   216
or shAun   !
sheM and
stEm
Stone beside the rivering waters

II

220   opal who having Jilted glugg is
         fAscinated by
           Miss
         corriE
           griSchun scoula bring the babes

221   Jests
            jOkes
interjection buckleY

222   musiC
           providEntially arranged by l'archet and laccorde

           dJowl
          releAsed
        shehind hiMs back

223   shE
           Shuffering all the diseasinesses of the

       melmelode Jawr
up tighty in the frOnt down again on the loose drim and drumming
         Yoe
        with searCh a fling
        did diE near sea

224   he was an inJine ruber
         Aunts to give
        whoM
        inhEbited
      hehry antletS on him

225   ploung Jamn
        his spOkes
         mitzYmitzy though i did ate
     van diemen's Coral
        pEarl

othersites of Jorden 228
heAve a hevy
tinsaMmon
till farthEr 229
alterS

send Jarge
and daunt yOu logh
if his vineshankY's
inform to the old sniggering publiCking
prEss and its nation of sheepcopers

he would Jused sit it
All write down just as
in hyMns
ignorancE
Seeing how heartsilly sorey he was

was liffe worth leaving neJ 230
thOledoth treetrene
pumme if Yell
while itCh ish 231
shomE

haveaJube
sillAyass joshua croesus
seed of suMm
aftEr at he had
breaStplates

Jerk
a ladle brOom jig
isle wail for Yews 232
Cap
twillEd a twine of flame

arrahbeeJee 234
hAppy
little girlycuMs
adolphtEd
Such

glycering Juwells lydialight fans and 236
le mOnade
sing a song of singlemonth and You'll too and
Chours
so comE on ye wealthy gentrymen

theJ olly
missAl too
push the puMkik round
annEliuia.
Since the days of roamaloose and rehmoose

238
like Juneses
nutslOst'
like the blue of the skY if i stoop for to spy's
between my whiteyoumightCallimbs how
makEs their triel eer's wax for

240
pure blood Jebusite
drugmAllt storehuse
sMily skibluh
Eye
alioS

242
so she not swop her eckcot hJem
hOwarden's castle englandwales
243
as hundreads elskerelks' Yahrds of annams
faCtory
frEsh and fuming at the mouth

245
the width of the way for Jogjoy hulker's cieclest elbownunsense
his dithering dAthering waltzers of
jeMpson's
wEed
deckS

−246
de oud huis biJ de kerkegaard
whOopee
saucY ·
Campus calls
girls arE merchand

Jerkoff
eAtsoup
yeM or yan
whilE
felixed iS who culpas does and harm's worth healing

253
splitten up or recompounded an isaac Jacquemin
maurOmormo milesian how ›
254
three stout sweYnhearts
of the orgiasts meeresChal macmuhun
Extremes giving quotidients to our means

bier wiJn   256
    Advokaat withouten pleaders
    Mas marrit pas poulit ras
is huEd
of each'S colour

lukkedoerendunandurraskewdylooshoofermoyportertooryzooysphalnabortansporthaokansakroidverJkapakkapuk   257
upplOud
    Youd   258
hear us loud graCiously
    hEar us

    Judges   263
    gAy lutharius
    Month with   264
    thrEe
    Saturnine settings

lead us seek o June   266
    thOu who fleeest
    thYself
    attaCh
with thinE efteased ensuer a question of

the law of the Jungerl   268
    eArly
    jeMmijohns
will cudgEl
browne and nolan'S divisional tables

    of Jemenfichue will sit and knit
halfwayhOist
    pYgmyhop a washable
love by seCond   269
    prudE

    Jeg suis
    thou Arr
    M. 50–50
    οὐκ"Ελαβον πόλιν
cookcook Search me

273
mangay mumbo Jumbjubes
mutts and jeffs muchas bracelOnettes
274
death raY stop him
entre Chats
dundErhead

.   .

big gleaming Jelly
for good vAunty years
275
in any large luMps
gEek
got the Strong of it

.   ͨ

into Jinglish janglage
dOlphins ,
276
babeteasing us out of our hoYdenname
sate with beCchus zumbock   ?   .
achEvre

,

279   ,
)   Jr
my lifstAck
to piMp   !
my impEnding marriage ,
nature tellS everybody

280
`.
la Jambe de marche
suppOsed adeal
shall plaY
her sideCurls
latEr

.   .
)
281
aux Jours
des bAtailles
blottoM
warE   .
trifid tongueS you daredevil donnelly

282   ˋ
,
hooJahs
kOojahs up
his fanden's catachYsm
Caiuscounting
.   in the scalE of pin puff pive piff piff puff pive

290
par Jure
you plAit nuncandtunc and
Mams
spottpricE
i   ,
twaS he was

in Juwelietry 291
kickychOses and madornaments
and mYrtle
at the reCtory
vicaragE road

! Jup 294
off cArpenger strate
with olaf as centruM
cyclonE allow
makefearSome's ocean you've actuary entducked one

kapitayn killyhook and the Jukes 295
private prOperties
a night of thoughtsendYures and a day
in effeCt
yulEs gone by

a gouvernament Job 301
moAnday tearsday
thuMpsday
fEar of the law
look at thiS twitches

low Jure 302
lOved to see
the macbeths jerseYs
knaCking spots of
Eagles sweet

last line from smith-Jones-orbison
yeArs
jirryaliMpaloop
hup u bn gd grl lifp yEar
fendS you all and moe

twofold truth and the conJunctive appetites 305
Oppositional orexes
roYally toobally
thou in shanty thou in sCanty shanty   thou in slanty scanty shanty
bidE in your hush bide in your hush

Julius 306
cAesar
cheMistry
disciplinE
at the South city markets belief in giants

308   new yonks from Jake jack
                             and little sOusoucie

         ,

         ˬ

                                        ,

310   patent number 1132 thorpetersen and synds Jomsborg selverbergen
                         twintriodic singulvAlvulous
                                tyMpan
                         bauliaughaclEeagh
                culpable of cunduncing naul and Santry

            or one watthour bilaws below till time Jings
                          hOst
                  indtil the teller oYne of an oustman in skull of skand
             when he pullupped the turfeyCork by
                          grEats of gobble out of lougk neagk

312   rotary Jewr
                      plebs but plAbs
313   consistently blown to adaMs
                        so hElp me boyg
                    who keepS the book

315   nogeysokey first cabootle segund Jilling
                       that Oerasound
                    the snarstY weg for publin so was his
                him how the hitCh did do this
                 my fand sulkErs

317   he apullaJibed
                       dAn so
                       Mansk
                   likE a dun darting dullemitter with
                   Stuck in plostures

318   Jilt the spin
                  and jOlt
                  a buoY
                   lowCasts
                    atEn of aimilikan

                stuff interJoked   320
                    boAth
                    scaMptail
                        irE wackering from the eyewinker
                    maSttop and aye far he fared

with winkles whelks and cocklesent Jelks   321
                    lit by night in the phOenix music
            contrescene he cupped his Years
                    to Catch
                    mE's to you

                    torstaJ   325
                    tAnssia
    lavantaj ja sunnuntaj christianisMus kirjallisuus kirjallisuus christianismus
                    this pEllover
                    finniSch

                    Jest   331
                    crOwn
                    the ketYl and   332
                    heC
                    lovE alpy

                and the Juinnesses is   333
                    rApin his hind
                    the Missus
                    braggEd abouve that
            her agony Stays outsize her

    it pickles up the punchey and the Jude   334
                    yOu'll
                        Yule to the day and it's hey tallaght hoe
                    Cup
                    it tEllyhows its story to   335

                    Jukersmen   337
                sure to pAltipsypote
                your fingathuMbs
                    hEahear
                    Solowly

                aJaculate all lea light   338
            rassamble the glOwrings
                of bruYant
                    Ching
                    lEw mang

339
come alleyou Jupes of wymmingtown
grAze the calves of
heavenspawn consoMation
rEnt outraged
erminia'S

340
dJublian alps
and the hOofd ribeiro
nYe
reguleCt
wifE in the rut of

his muJiksy's
zAravence
341
act which seeMs
to sharpnEl
innermalS menody

342
gross Jumpiter whud was thud
hOld hard
major hermYn
reproduCing
form of famous sirEs on the scene of the formers triumphs

343
poJr
schtschuptAr
all the qwehrMin
of thosE
antiantS their grandoper that soun of a gunnong

344
i confesses withould prideJealice
when i lOoked
345
at Yarn's length
by wile of stoCcan his hand and of
gEtting umptyums gatherumed off

348
a great mark for Jinking
brocAde for
a burM
whEm
it bameS fire

351
blue streak Jisty and pithy
as hOmard
(kaYenne was
Choplain
bluEd

his bigotes bristling as Jittinju triggity shittery pet   352
he shouts his thump and feeh fAuh foul finngures up
the frustate fourstar russkakruscaM dom allaf
of sin prakticE   353
failing to furrow theogonieS of the dommed

loud lauds to his luckhump and beJetties   358
jOnahs and
tombuYs disassembling and taking him apart   !
the slammoCks
with discrimination for his maypolE and

what we warn to hear Jeff is the woods of chirpsies cries   359
sock him up the oldcAnt rogue group a you have jest
a haM
bEamed
liStening through

grootvatter lodewiJk   361
bOldmans
You're
the jangtherapper of all joColarinas
and thEy were as were they

rosing he Jumps   363
leAps rizing
he's their Mark
cErtainty owe
he Sprit in his phiz

e'en tho' Jambuwel's defecalties is   366
sippahsedly imprOctor
marse makes a good daYle to be shattat
jaCq jacob's
griEf

k.c. Jowls   368
they sure Are wise
Mr g.b.   369
hilly gapE
mr w.k. ferriS-fender fert fort woovil doon

Jameseslane   373
begetting a wife which begame his niece by pOuring
her Youngthings into skintighs
it Crops out
in your flEsh   374

375   you on her hosy Jigses
                           thAt'll be
                     fuMmuccumul
                with a granEen aveiled
            playing down the Slavey touch

376   Jik
                 yOu're getting hoovier a twelve stone hoovier
           and the greY
                   Club too with
                wEre for the massus for to feed

383   and they kemin in so hattaJocky only
384   quArtebuck askull for
            old Matt,
              grEgory
          and then beSides old matt there was

386   Jules
            with the hOughers
               Yaman and all the
−387   priesthunters from the Curragh
            and confusionariEs and the authorities

     and his crimson harness and his leathern Jib
               his cheApshein hairshirt
            that reMinds
               mE
         about the manauSteriums of the poor

   then there was the official landing of lady Jales casemate in the year
              the flOod 1132 s.o.s.
      and then poor merkin cornYngwham
            the offiCial out of
              pEnsion when

394   Jool
            the rAncers
          egotuM
               dEprofundity
       of multimathematical immaterialitieS

tootwoly torrific the mummurrlubeJubes 396

cOunting motherpeributts up one up four

in lethargY's love at the end of it all 397

Caxons

wEt air register

III

prAties sweet and irish too

and Mock

gurglE

to whiStle his way through for the swallying

burud and dulse and typureely Jam all free of charge aman and

lOaves are

quaY (

lynCh

hE's deeply draiming houseanna

take this John's 408

lAne in your toastingfourch shaunti

and shaunti again and twelve coolinder Moons i am

studiEd

piScisvendolor you're grace futs dronk

tackling bienie faith as well and Jucking 417

dOrsan

in the mYre

aCtually

and prEsumptuably sinctifying chronic's despair

31 Jun. 13 421

12 p.d. rAzed

cuMm

camE

Stop

422   he can purge his contempt and deJeunerate

                a skillytOn be thinking himself to death

          if he waits till i buY him a mosselman's present

         ho's nos halfCousin

            of minE pigdish nor wants

423   went into the society of Jewses

              with bro cAhlls and

424   teMp

            whEn he foiled

           the *ikiSh*

430   girlsfuss over him pellmale their *Jeune premier*

           mussing his frizzy hAir

              siMply savouring

        wiḷd thymE

        and parSley

             Jaun asking kindlily

       are bernadetta's cOlumbillas

431   coY

            a bittoCk

            a sidEeye

      from sampson's tyke to Jones's   *i*

           sprAt

    jaun after those few preliMbs

         iknowEd

          her waveS of splabashing and she showed him proof

435   always Jaeger

              mOedl's with their

          danuboYes

             stiCk wicks

             whEn you hear the prompter's voice

441   the race is to the rashest of the romping Jomping rushes of

              hAul seton's

         ad libidinuM

        if you'vE

           parentS and things to look after

divulge sJuddenly
   jOuted out hardworking jaun
   braYing aloud like brahaam's
   kinantiCs
   in that buEl of gruel he gobed at bedgo

what do you mean by Jno   447
   jAs pagan
   traM
    wEaring the midlimb
   veStee

     Jushed astunshed   448
durn weel tOpcoated with
   tristYs blinking   449
  and jaCobus
  intErcissous

as a philopotamus and crekking Jugs
   grenoulls leAving tealeaves for the trout
  westasleep aMuckst
to watch how carEfully
   nocturnal gooSemother would lay her new golden sheegg   −450

   bemolly and Jiesis
    i spOrt a
    brYony o'bryony
  what sensitive Coin
    possEssed

neck and necklike derby and June to our snug   454
   retribution's rewArd the scorchhouse shunt us
saffron buns or sovran bonhaMs   455
   whichEver you'r avider
  allover irelandS

and a penny in the plate for the Jemes   456
   O.k oh
   Yon
   Coat of
 vairy furry bEst i'll try and pullll it awn mee

  the Jooks
the kelly-cooks hAve
   Milking
  marshalsEa
 i   firSt offenders but i know what i'll do

458   i will tie a knot in my stringameJip
                  it will be wOrth
                      simplY and solely
                         Comb and mirror   i
                      owEs and artless awes

465   hatch yourself well enJombyourselves thurily
                  would you wAit biss she buds till you
                             Mails
                         togEther
                      like the corkS again brothers hungry and angry

469   Jerne
                      abOard for kew
               solong lood erYnnana ware thee wail
                      now's nunC
                      or nimmEr

470   eh Jourd'weh oh jourd'woe
                      to-mAronite's
               oasis cedarous esaltershoMing
                         lEafboughnoon
                         oiSis

       half a glance of irish frisky a Juan jaimesan
                      hastaluegO
471   sososopkY
                      peoCchia
                         pEucchia ho mi hoping ha me happinice

                      borne of bJoerne
                         lA garde
                      coos hogdaM
                         farvEl
                         Speed

473   spatched fun Juhn
                  that dandyfOrth from the night we are and feel and
                      phaYnix
                         Cock shall crow
                      wEst shall shake the east awake walk

oh Jeyses fluid 480
sAys the poisoned well
did you dreaM you
ating your own tripE
acuShla that you tied yourself up

scents and gouspils the animal Jangs again
hOwl me wiseacre's hat till
Yu hald 481
Chris
drEam

your stavrotides Jong of 482
mAho
and that o'Mulanchonry
no usE
donkeySchott

every other woman has a Jape in her 486
fellOw
o seY but swift and
bellax aCting
likE a bellax

when a crispin sokolist besoops Juts 491
or clApperclaws
Mum
a drary lanE
juSt hadded twinned little curls

i am writing in mepetition to kavanagh dJanaral when he 492
as badazmy emOtional volvular
with vallad of erill pearceY o 493
in my nil ensemble in his lazyChair
up my hEmifaces in all my mayarannies

alas for livings' pledJures 496
lordy dAw and lady don
boycotted and girlcutted in debt and dooM
on hill and havEn
even by·the Show-the-flag flotilla

watersheads and to change that subJunct
Once in a while
identifY yourself with the him in you
fluCtuous
nEck merchamtur

503   all effects in their Joints
                          cAused ways
                        toMbs
                      dEep and heavy
                and what Sigeth woodin warneung thereof

511   the other men Jazzlike
                      brOllies and sesuos was gickling his missus
                    beYawnd
                tweendeCks
                  dEeply painfully

                    Junk
                the jungulAr
512 life out of the liffey crestofer caraMbas such is zodisfaction you
                    kishEd he conquered
                      muSked bell of this masked ball

514   making meJical
                    shOw in sum some
                  claY
                    Cast
              through the schappstEckers of hoy's house

524   mr coppinger hereckons himself disJunctively
                  with his windwArrd eye
                    a cunifarM school of
                      nazE from twelve and them
             mayridinghim by the Silent hour butting charging bracing

531   me shims and here's me hams and this is me Juppettes gause be the meter
                  he never cOtched finer
                    by sYlph and salamander and
                primapatrioCk of
                trancEnania

532   Jousters of the king
                  eirenArch's custos
                in pontofacts Massimust
           throughout the world whErever
                good allengliSches angleslachsen is spoken

533   from an early peepee period while still to hedJe-
                      skOol intended for broadchurch i
                have the phoneY habit
             saywhen holmstoCk
                unstEaden

                    a bloweyed laneJoymt   !   534
                              fAllse roude axehand he is
                         thoM's
                         snakEeye
                              Strangler of
hanging tower steck a Javelin
                         thrOugh his advowtried heart
                         chrY as urs now so yous then   535
                         first City's
                              lEasekuays

                    i cast my tenspan Joys on her   547
                              Arsched overtupped
what screech of shippings what low of daMpfbulls   −548
         from livland hoks zivios fromNEttland
                              Skall vives with impress of asias and

                    knaggs of Jets
              and silvered waterrOses
          the peak of pim's and slYne's
                    a sChool
                    of shElls of moyles marine

              and piebald shJelties   554
                    skewbAld
                    doMino

                         Jot   563
                    sobrAt
         steelwhite and blackMail i ha'scint
                         for my swEet
              an anemone'S letter with a gold of my bridest hair betied

                         kerryJevin
                         a seçOnd position   564
                         of sYlvious beltings
                    are to be Caught
                         a scarlEt pimparnell

Writing for the Second Time through Finnegans Wake : 173

565   gaiJ beutel

                               of stAub to feel

                             the tiMid

                             vortigErn ah

                                     Stemming   what boyazhness

568   me amble dooty to your grace's maJers

                     we but miss that hOrse elder

                             alfi bYrni

                                 eaCla

                                   trEacla youghta kaptor lomdom noo

571   hedJes of

                                  mAiden

                               ferM

                                 hEre in another place

                           chapelofeaSes

578   and her steptoJazyma's culunder buzztle

                  selling sunlit sOpes to washtout winches and

                             stepneY's

579   eskipping the Clockback, crystal

                           swEeteheartedly

583   lickering Jessup

                           bAtter

               she druv behind her stuMps for a

             wink through his tunnilclEfft

                       bagSlops

590   Jeebies ugh

                      jawbOose puddigood

                       Yond would be

               worked out to an inCh

                     his corE

IV

616   by Jings
with the greAtest
hairy of chest haMps and
         affEctionate company
real devoteS

620   hugly Judsys what
chOose is left to
Yearns

621   nor you your ruCksunck
hikE

622   round the lodge of fJorn
gAlla
taMming
unclE
tim'S caubeen

626   as on the night of the apophanypes Jumpst
shOotst throbbst into me mouth like
us two onlY i was but teen
a pining Child round
sluppEry table

i'm sure he squirted Juice in his eyes
to mAke
theM flash
for flightEning me
Still and all he was awful fond to me

627   Just a whisk
Of
pitY
a Cloud
in pEace and silence

This text is a revision of an earlier one finished in 1974 which was given as a lecture at the YMHA in New York City and printed in *Numus West*, No. 5–74.

The Future of Music

For many years I've noticed that music—as an activity separated from the rest of life—doesn't enter my mind. Strictly musical questions are no longer serious questions.

It wasn't always that way. When I was setting out to devote my life to music, there still were battles to win within the field of music. People distinguished between musical sounds and noises. I followed Varèse and fought for noises. Other musicians also did. In the early thirties the only piece for percussion alone was Varèse's *Ionisation*. By 1942 there were over one hundred such works. Now they are countless. Almost anyone who listens to sound now listens easily no matter what overtone structures the sounds have. We no longer discriminate against noises.

We can also hear any pitch, whether or not it's part of a scale of one temperament or another, occidental or oriental. Sounds formerly considered out of tune are now called microtones. They are part and parcel of modern music.

Some people still object to loud sounds. They're afraid of hurting their ears. Once I had the opportunity to hear a very loud sound (the conclusion of a Zaj performance). I'd been in the audience the evening before. I knew when the sound was coming. I moved close to the loudspeaker from which it was to be heard and sat there for an hour, turning first one ear and then the other toward it. When it stopped, my ears were ringing. The ringing continued through the night, through the next day, and through the next night. Early the following day I made an appointment with an ear specialist. On my way to his office, the ringing seemed to have more or less subsided. The doctor made a thorough examination, said my ears were normal. The disturbance had been temporary. My attitude toward loud sounds has not changed. I shall listen to them whenever I get the chance, keeping perhaps a proper distance.

Our experience of time has changed. We notice brief events that formerly might have escaped our notice and we enjoy very long ones, ones having lengths that would have been considered, say fifteen years ago, intolerable.

Nor are we concerned about how a sound begins, continues, and dies away. During a panel discussion on piano music from the People's Republic of China, Chou Wen-

Chung said that Western musicians formerly insisted that a pitched sound should stay on pitch, not waver from the moment it begins until it ends. Chinese musicians, he said, feel some change in its course in its pitch enlivens a sound, makes it "musical." Nowadays, anyone listens to any sounds, no matter how flexible or inflexible they are with respect to any of their characteristics. We've become attentive to sounds we've never heard before. I was fascinated when Lejaren Hiller described his project to use computer means to make a "fantastic orchestra," to synthesize extraordinary sounds, sounds beginning as though plucked, continuing as from pipes, ending as though bowed.

We're also open-minded about silence. Silence isn't as generally upsetting as it used to be.

And melody. *Klangfarbenmelodie* has not taken the place of *bel canto*. It has extended our realization of what can happen. The same is true of aperiodic rhythm: it includes the possibility of periodic rhythm. Two or more lines composed of sounds can be heard whether they involve known or invented kinds of counterpoint or are just simultaneous (not intervallically controlled). Even if two melodies, one very loud, the other very soft, are played at the same time, we know if we listen carefully, or from another position in space, we'll hear them both.

We can be extremely careful about harmony, as Lou Harrison, La Monte Young, and Ben Johnston are, or we can be, as I often am, extremely careless about harmony. Or we can make do as our orchestras do with grey compromise about which sounds sounded together are harmonious.

Anything goes. However, not everything is attempted. Take the division of a whole into parts. In the 'thirties I was impressed by Schoenberg's insistence on musical structure, but disagreed with his view that tonality was its necessary means. I investigated time-lengths as a more comprehensive means. Using permutation, I made tables of the numbers one through twelve, giving their division into prime numbers. These number-series could be understood either in terms of tonality or time-length or rhythmic structures. The series 1-2-1, which appears in the table for the number 4, can be recognized as an A-B-A structure. It could be expressed tonally or rhythmically (or both). The number 7 has 64 different number-series. Only three of these are A-B-A, namely, 2-3-2, 3-1-3, and 1-5-1. Though some of the others have been exemplified musically, I think many have not. The possibilities increase for the higher numbers. There are 2,048 for the number 12. If we add the possibility of fractions, who knows what musical structures may be discovered? Interesting ones are being found by Elliott Carter and Conlon Nancarrow involving superimposed independent gradual transitions from one tempo to another; those by Nancarrow are particularly interesting. Dealing exclusively with player pianos, he produces extremes of speed that are astonishing and exhilarating.

Many composers no longer make musical structures. Instead they set processes going. A structure is like a piece of furniture, whereas a process is like the weather. In the case of a table, the beginning and end of the whole and each of its parts are known. In the case of weather, though we notice changes in it, we have no clear knowledge of its beginning or ending. At a given moment, we are when we are. The nowmoment.

Were a limit to be set to possible musical processes, a process outside that limit would surely be discovered. Since processes can include objects (be analogous, that is, to environment), we see there is no limit. For some time now, I have preferred processes to objects for just this reason: processes do not exclude objects. It doesn't work the other way around. Within each object, of course, a lively molecular process is in operation. But if we are to hear it, we must isolate the object in a special chamber. To focus attention, one must ignore all the rest of creation. We have a history of doing precisely that. In changing our minds, therefore, we look for that attitude that is non-exclusive, that can include what we know together with what we do not yet imagine.

There is the question of feelings, whether like emotions they seem to come spontaneously from within, or, like likes and dislikes, they seem to be caused by sense perceptions. In either case, we know that life's more fully lived when we are open to whatever—that life is minimized when we protect ourselves from it. Naturally, we don't set out to kill ourselves. We will continue to "wrestle with the Daimonic" (as M. C. Richards puts it), and a variety of disciplines will continue to be used to open the mind to events beyond its control. But more and more a concern with personal feelings of individuals, even the enlightenment of individuals, will be seen in the larger context of society. We know how to suffer or control our emotions. If not, advice is available. There is a cure for tragedy. The path to self-knowledge has been mapped out by psychiatry, by oriental philosophy, mythology, occult thought, anthroposophy, and astrology. We know all we need to know about Oedipus, Prometheus, and Hamlet. What we are learning is how to be convivial. "Here Comes Everybody." Though the doors will always remain open for the musical expression of personal feelings, what will more and more come through is the expression of the pleasures of conviviality (as in the music of Terry Riley, Steve Reich, and Philip Glass). And beyond that a nonintentional expressivity, a being together of sounds and people (where sounds are sounds and people are people). A walk, so to speak, in the woods of music, or in the world itself.

The difference between closed-mindedness and open-mindedness resembles the difference between the critical and creative faculties, or the difference between information about something (or knowledge even) and that something itself. Christian Wolff found the following, written by Charles Ives, and sent it on to me: "What music is and is to be may be somewhere in the belief of an unknown philosopher of half a century ago who said, 'How can there be any bad music? All music is from heaven. If there is anything bad in it, I put it there—by my implications and limitations. Nature builds the mountains and meadows and man puts in the fences and labels.'" The fences have come down and the labels are being removed. An up-to-date aquarium has all the fish swimming together in one huge tank.

Musical open-mindedness has come about in this century in Europe both West and East, in the Americas, in Japan, Australia, and perhaps New Zealand. It doesn't exist, except perhaps exceptionally, in India, Indonesia, and Africa. (When in traveling around the world with the Dance Company in 1964 we came to India, Merce Cunningham said, "This is the land of the future.") Musical open-mindedness exists in Russia but is not permitted exportation. It is politically excluded in China (though I've heard tell that sometime in the 'sixties Italy's representatives in China managed to arrange a concert in Peking of the music of Sylvano Bussotti).

The reasons for this musical open-mindedness are several. First of all: the activities, the battles won, by many composers. In this country alone, open-mindedness is implied by the work particularly of Ives, Ruggles, Cowell, and Varèse. Cowell used to tell the story about Ruggles and the Florida class in harmony. The problem of modulating from one key to another "very distant" one was discussed. After an hour, the instructor asked Ruggles how he, Ruggles, would solve the problem. Ruggles said: I wouldn't make a problem out of it; I'd just go from one to the other without any transition.

A second reason for open-mindedness: changes in technology associated with music. Given the tape recorders, synthesizers, sound systems, and computers we have, we could not reasonably have been expected to keep our minds fixed on the music of earlier centuries, even though many of the schools, conservatories, and music critics still do. A third reason for open-mindedness: the interpenetration of cultures formerly separated. In the nineteenth century even Englishmen occupying India were few and far between who took Indian music seriously. Times have changed. At the present time, if a university takes music seriously, it does as Wesleyan University in Connecticut does: it brings together in one school as many different musical cultures of the world as it can afford (music of Africa, of India, of Indonesia, and Japan, together with European music, music of the American Indians, and new electronic music). A fourth reason for open-mindedness: there are more of us and we have many ways of getting together (the telephone, the media, travel by air). If one of us doesn't have an idea that will open the minds of the rest of us, another will. We begin to be keenly aware of the richness and uniqueness of each individual and the natural capacity in each person to open up new possibilities for another. In her recent book, *The Crossing Point*, M. C. Richards tells of her work with retarded children, how it is characterized not just by her helping them, but also by their helping her. Some years ago I was asked to speak to a group of doctors associated with a mental hospital in Connecticut. I had no clear idea in my mind what to say. But as I went down the corridors toward the room where I was to speak, I found myself among people "out of their minds." What had to be said to the doctors became clear: You're sitting on top of a gold mine! Share the wealth with the rest of us! The same is true of our prisons. When Buckminster Fuller did not know whether his wife Anne was to live or not (following an automobile accident), or, if she did live, whether she would be incapacitated or not, it was a letter from a former convict in a California penitentiary on the subject of life, love, and death that gave him consolation. There are untouched resources in children and teen-agers which we do not have because we send them to school; and among the military whom we lose by sending them around the world and beneath its surface to bomb-proof offensive installations; and among the senior citizens whom we have persuaded to leave us in favor of sunshine, fun, and games. We have systematically deprived ourselves of all these people, probably because we didn't want them to bother us while we were doing whatever we were doing. But if there is any experience more than another which conduces to open-mindedness, it is the experience of being bothered by another, of being interrupted by another. "We are studying being interrupted." Say we do not practice any spiritual discipline. The telephone then does it for us. It opens us to the world "outside."

George Herbert Mead said that when one is very young he feels he belongs to one family, not to any other. As he grows older, he belongs to one neighborhood rather than another: later, to one nation rather than another. When he feels no limit to that to which he belongs, he has, Mead said, developed the religious spirit. The open-mindedness among composers (which has affected performers and listeners too) is comparable and kin to the religious spirit. The religious spirit must now become social so that all Mankind is seen as Family, Earth as Home. Music's ancient purpose—to sober and quiet the mind, thus making it susceptible to divine influences—is now to be practiced in relation to the Mind of which through technological extension we all are part, a Mind, these days, confused, disturbed, and split.

Music has already taken steps in this direction, toward social interaction, the non-political togetherness of people.

The Renaissance-honored distinctions between composers, performers, and listeners are no longer everywhere maintained. The blurring of these distinctions has come about for several reasons. First of all: the activities of many composers, particularly Feldman and Wolff, who have made their compositions indeterminate, so that performers, rather than merely doing what they are told to do, have the opportunity to use their own faculties, to make decisions in a field of possibilities, to cooperate, that is, in a particular musical undertaking. Those listening to indeterminate music have been encouraged in their listening, since they have been joined in such music by the composers and performers too.

Secondly, technology has brought about the blurring of the distinctions between composers, performers, and listeners. Just as anyone feels himself capable of taking a photograph by means of a camera, so now and increasingly so in the future anyone, using recording and/or electronic means, feels and will increasingly feel himself capable of making a piece of music, combining in his one person the formerly distinct activities of composer, performer, and listener. However, to combine in one person these several activities is, in effect, to remove from music its social nature. It is the social nature of music, the practice in it of using a number of people doing different things to make it, that distinguishes it from the visual arts, draws it toward theater, and makes it relevant to society, even society outside musical society. The popularity of recordings is unfortunate, not only for musical reasons, but for social reasons: it permits the listener to isolate himself from other people. What is needed is not that the several activities of different people come together in one person, but that the distinctions between the roles of different people be blurred, so that they themselves may come together.

A third cause for the blurring of the distinctions between composers, performers, and listeners: the interpenetration of cultures formerly separated. There is no longer an essential difference between some serious music and some popular music—or, you may say, a bridge exists between them: their common use of the same sound systems, the same microphones, amplifiers, and loudspeakers. In the cases of much popular and some oriental musics, the distinctions between composers and performers were never very clear. Notation, as Busoni said it did, did not stand between musician and music. People simply came together and made music. Improvisation. It can take place, so to speak, strictly, as within the *raga* and *tala* limitations of Indian music, or it can take place freely, merely in a space of time, as sounds do environmentally, whether in the country or in the cities. Just as aperiodic rhythm can include periodic rhythm, just as process can include object, so free improvisations can include strict ones, can even include compositions. The Jam Session. The Musicircus.

In 1974 Richard K. Winslow suggested changing my instrumental parts for *Etcetera* so that they would read Bowed Instrument, Wind Instrument, Double Reed, Single Reed, rather than Violin, Flute, Oboe, Clarinet, thus bringing to parts for pitched instruments something of the vagueness and freedom conventionally given to parts for percussion players. (If you don't have the percussion instrument called for, you substitute something else.) Oriental and occidental instruments together in ensemble. A duet between tuba and sitar! This is possible only when the actions to be made are not on the ground special to either, but on the ground common to both. Since *Etcetera*, I have written *Score with Parts: Twelve Haiku* and *Renga*, graphic notations in which the parts are differentiated only by numbers. A given part may be played on any instrument.

With our increase in population there has come about a great increase in musical activity. Formerly concerts of new music were few and far between. Now there is more going on than you can shake a stick at. So that it always surprises me when I run into the thought there's nothing further, nothing new, to do in music; though I remember feeling that way in the early 'thirties: I was full of admiration for what had been accomplished; I had not yet gotten to work. For the most part, music that's now being made in New York, the new music, that is, is music I want to hear, though too often I cannot for I'm busy elsewhere. Audiences are large, generally filling the spaces used. And more and more, as in the evenings in New York known as "Sounds out of Silent Spaces," evenings with a cooperative music-making group founded by Philip Corner, the audiences themselves participate.

We can say that this blurring of the distinctions between composers, performers, and listeners is evidence of an ongoing change in society, not only in the structure of society, but in the feelings that people have for one another. Fear, guilt, and greed associated with hierarchical societies are giving way to mutual confidence, a sense of common well-being, and a desire to share with another whatever one person happens to have or to do. However, these changed social feelings which characterize many evenings of new music do not characterize the society as a whole.

Revolution remains our proper concern. But instead of planning it, or stopping what we're doing in order to do it, it may be that we are at all times in it. I quote from M. C. Richards' book, *The Crossing Point:* "Instead of revolution being considered exclusively as an attack from outside upon an established form, it is being considered as a potential resource—an art of transformation voluntarily undertaken from within. Revolution arm in arm with evolution, creating a balance which is neither rigid nor explosive. Perhaps we will learn to relinquish voluntarily our patterns of power and subservience, and work together for organic change."

At the beginning of the *Essay on Civil Disobedience*, Thoreau has this quotation: "That government is best which governs not at all." He adds: "And when men are prepared for it, that will be the kind of government which they will have." Many musicians are ready. We now have many musical examples of the practicality of anarchy. Music with indeterminate parts, no fixed relation of them (no score). Music without notation. Our rehearsals are not conducted. We use that time to make our setups: to make sure that everything that is needed by any of the musicians is there, that everything is in good working order. Musicians can do without government. Like ripe fruit (I refer to the metaphor at the end of Thoreau's *Essay*), they have dropped away from the tree.

Less anarchic kinds of music give examples of less anarchic states of society. The masterpieces of Western music exemplify monarchies and dictatorships. Composer and conductor: king and prime minister. By making musical situations which are analogies to desirable social circumstances which we do not yet have, we make music suggestive and relevant to the serious questions which face Mankind.

Some politically concerned composers do not so much exemplify in their work the desired changes in society as they use their music as propaganda for such changes or as criticism of the society as it continues insufficiently changed. This necessitates the use of words. Sounds by themselves do not put messages across. And when they do not use words, politically concerned composers tend to revert to nineteenth-century musical practices. This is enforced in both Russia and China. And encouraged in England by Cornelius Cardew and the members of the Scratch Orchestra. They study the pronouncements on art by Mao Tse-tung and apply them as literally and legalistically as they can. They therefore have criticized the politically concerned music of Frederick Rjewski and Christian Wolff, simply because new ways to make music have been discovered by both of these composers. Rjewski's works (and some of Garrett List's, too) flow like the rapids of a river: they suggest irresistible change. Rjewski and List have found virtuosi who vocalize rapidly and over long periods of time uninterruptedly (not seeming to take any time off to breathe); Wolff's works invariably reveal to both performers and listeners energy resources they have of which they hadn't been aware and put those energies intelligently to work.

Implicit in the use of words (when messages are put across) are training, government, enforcement, and finally the military. Thoreau said that hearing a sentence he heard feet marching. Syntax, N. O. Brown told me, is the arrangement of the army. The pen has formerly been considered more powerful than the sword. American shame and spiritual frustration result at least in part from the fact that even though the country's best pens and best voices throughout our history have been raised in protest against our government's actions, and even though thorough plans have been clearly proposed for the improvement of environment and the well-being of all people—not just Americans, but all people—the American powers that be remain deaf and blind. We know from Buckminster Fuller and many others that the continued use of fossil fuels is against both environment and the lives of people in it. We should use above-earth energy sources exclusively: sun, wind, tides, and algae. The nations don't seem to know this. National and international triumphs, whether of the USA or other countries, still have to do with the foolish exploitation of below-earth resources. Fuller did not smile when I asked him about atomic energy. Inevitable in it is the slow but steady raising of Earth's temperature to a heat in which life would be unendurable (see Robert L. Heilbroner: *An Inquiry into the Human Prospect*). Since words, when they communicate, have no effect, it dawns on us that we need a society in which communication is not practiced, in which words become nonsense as they do between lovers, in which words become what they originally were: trees and stars and the rest of primeval environment. The demilitarization of language: a serious musical concern.

When I was commissioned by the Boston Symphony Orchestra to write a work in celebration of the American Bicentennial, Seiji Ozawa said, "Make it easy!" Our institutions, not just the musical ones, are incapable of hard work. Time is counted to the second and limited. The goal of an individual within an institution has nothing to do with the work to be done or with the state of his mind. It has to do with the payment to be received. A necessary aspect of the immediate future, not just in the field of environmental recovery, is work, hard work, and no end to it. Much of my music since 1974 is extremely difficult to play (the *Etudes Australes* for the pianist Grete Sultan; the *Freeman Etudes* for the violinist Paul Zukofsky). The overcoming of difficulties. Doing the impossible. Grete Sultan was enthusiastic at the prospect of work. When I told the composer Garrett List what I was up to, there was liveliness in his eyes and a smile of recognition. He also was at work on something having the nature of work. And a recent long work by Christian Wolff is called *Exercises*.

Tom Howell at the University of Illinois inspired his students to explore the playing of two or more notes at a time on a single wind instrument. In the books you can play only one at a time: His teaching produced work. Multiphonics.

As a pianist, David Tudor laboriously developed the ability, not yet approached by others, to give each attack in a rapid succession of many its own dynamic character. He took the principle underlying *Klangfarbenmelodie* (a succession of different timbres) and applied it to the relation between himself and his instrument: differences of energy, of distance and speed of attack, an extension of the understanding of the mechanism of keys, hammers, strings. Nowadays, Tudor rarely plays the piano. His work is in the field of electronics, often in relation to video, and often in collaboration with others. He invents components and sound systems of great originality. He solders and constructs them. He keeps abreast of the developments throughout the world in the field of electronics. He makes new loudspeakers free of the constriction of high fidelity.

There is endless work to be done in the field of electronic music. And many people at work: David Behrman, Gordon Mumma, Robert Ashley, Alvin Lucier, Phill Niblock, to name five. And in the field of video and visual technology (composers also have eyes): Lowell Cross, Tony Martin, Nam June Paik, to name three. And in the field of computer music (shortly everyone, whether he's a musician or not, will have a computer in his pocket): Joel Chadabe, Giuseppe Englaert, Jean-Claude Risset, Lejaren Hiller, Max Mathews, John Chowning, Charles Dodge, Emmanuel Ghent, to name eight.

As I look back over my own work, I observe that more often than not I have had other people in mind. I had Robert Fizdale and Arthur Gold in mind when I wrote the *Book of Music for Two Pianos*. The *Sonatas and Interludes* for prepared piano is a portrait of Maro Ajemian. Beginning with my *Music of Changes*, and continuing through *Variations VI*, my music always had David Tudor in mind. I notice now that many composers in their work have not a person but a place (environment) in mind. This is true of Pauline Oliveros' work, *In Memoriam Nikola Tesla*. The concern with place characterizes the work of Alison Knowles, whether she is working with Yoshimasa Wada or Annea Lockwood. Music becomes something to visit. Or a shrine, as in the *Eternal Music* of La Monte Young. An environment to go through (as in a work by Maryanne Amacher, or Max Neuhaus, or Liz Phillips). At Wesleyan University I met two young men studying with Alvin Lucier, Ron Goldman and Nicolas Collins. They gave an electronic concert in the tunnels below the new Arts Center in Middletown. By walking through the tunnels one passed through nodes and noticed (as one does in Oliveros' work) sympathetic vibrations arising in the building and its furniture. There's music to be made in geodesic domes, on unused subway platforms, in laundromats, in fields, forests, and in cities conceived as Robert Moran conceives them as immense concert halls.

Sympathetic vibrations. Suggestiveness and work. I have heard electronic components go into operation even though they were not plugged into the system. I said to someone who understood electronics and who was helping me, "Don't you think that's strange? It's not connected but it's working." His comment: "It's so close to the others, I would find it stranger if it didn't start working."

People and places. Musical theater. The Happening. The longest one we've ever had (Watergate) is still going on (at least in our minds). It is comparable to Greek or Noh drama. I attended a very short happening (not more than two minutes). It was performed in the window of a coffee shop in Soho by Ralston Farina, a young man who changed his name when he noticed two boxes of cereal. The audience with coats on stood in the street outside. His work was enigmatic and invigorating.

People and places: ritual. People and places: food. I remember attending a Potlatch near Anacortes, Washington. For days and nights people under the same roof sleeping, eating, cooking, dancing, singing. Changing the USA so that it becomes American Indian again. Margaret Mead. Bob Wilson. Jerome Rothenberg. David McAllester. Avery Jimerson of the Seneca Tribe.

Buckminster Fuller's *Synergetics* (876 pages) was published in 1975. It is no doubt inspiring a new music.

Merce Cunningham's dancing is also inspiring. Through the years Cunningham's faithfulness to the principle of work has never wavered. His dance technique itself is not fixed. It is a continuing series of discoveries of what a human body can do when it moves in and through space. Sometimes he appears as someone who has an insatiable appetite for dance; at other times he seems like dance's slave. James Rosenberg, a young Berkeley, California, poet whose work I admire, makes of himself, as I advised him, a slave to poetry. He is inspired, as I am, by Jackson MacLow's example of untiring devotion. I recall a performance by Charlemagne Palestine that was reminiscent of the body-art of Vito Acconci. Palestine shouted a vocal music at high amplitude while continuously running at high speed through the audience for a long time up to the point of physical exhaustion.

The first part of a new text by Norman O. Brown is on work. It was his reaction, I believe, to the somewhat complacent, though religious, spirit of the young in California communes. The willingness to settle for survival. Brown's concern is how to make a new civilization. Work is the first chapter. Ideas are in the air. In our polluted air there is the idea that we must get to work. Somehow, recently, in New York and in other cities too, the air seems less polluted than it was. Work has begun.

For a musical work to be implemented in China, it must be proposed not by an individual but by a team. The necessity for teamwork in music has been emphasized by Pierre Boulez in a Canadian interview with him about the research institute, IRCAM, now formed at the Centre Pompidou in Paris. The evenings with Philip Corner, Emily Derr, Andrew Franck, Dan Goode, William Hellerman, Tom Johnson, Alison Knowles, Dika Newlin, Carole Weber, Julie Winter, and the participating "audience" are teamwork. They are learning how to work together without one person's telling another what to do, and these evenings are open to strangers. How many people can work together happily, not just efficiently—happily and unselfishly? A serious question which the future of music will help to answer.

When I received the announcement of the evenings with Philip Corner and his friends, I noticed that no names were given, not even Philip Corner's. However, the announcement was not typeset; it was handwritten. And I recognized Philip Corner's handwriting. The omission of names. Anonymity. People going underground. In order, like Duchamp, to get the work done that is to be done.

People frequently ask me what my definition of music is. This is it. It is work. That is my conclusion.

However, just as I wrote it, the doorbell rang. It was the postman bringing me a present from William McNaughton, his editing of *Chinese Literature* (an anthology from the earliest times to the present day). The book includes many of McNaughton's own translations. On the endpaper of my copy is a dedication to me followed by fourteen Chinese characters, a reference to page 121, and McNaughton's signature. I turned to page 121 and read the following from his translation of *Chuang-tzu's Book:* "Everybody knows that useful is useful, but nobody knows that useless is useful, too." This is from Chapter 4 of *Chuang-tzu's Book*. A tree is described that gives a great deal of shade. It was very old and had never been cut down simply because its wood was considered to be of no use to anyone.

I want to tell the story of Thoreau and his setting fire to the woods. I think it is relevant to the practice of music in the present world situation, and it may suggest actions to be taken as we move into the future.

First of all, he didn't mean to set the fire. (He was broiling fish he had caught.) Once it was beyond his control, he ran over two miles unsuccessfully for help. Since there was nothing he could do alone he walked to Fair Haven Cliff, climbed to the highest rock, and sat down upon it to observe the progress of the flames. It was a glorious spectacle and he was the only one there to see it. From that height he heard bells in the village sounding alarm. Until then he had felt guilty, but knowing that help was coming his attitude changed. He said to himself: "Who are these men who are said to be the owners of these woods, and how am I related to them? I have set fire to the forest, but I have done nothing wrong therein, and it is as if the lightning had done it. These flames are but consuming their natural food."

When the townsmen arrived to fight the fire, Thoreau joined them. It took several hours to subdue the flames. Over one hundred acres were burned. Thoreau noticed that the villagers were generally elated, thankful for the opportunity that had given them so much sport. The only unhappy ones were those whose property had been destroyed. However, one of the owners was obliged to ask Thoreau the shortest way home, even though the path went through the owner's own land.

Subsequently, Thoreau met a fellow who was poor, miserable, often drunk, worthless (a burden to society). However, more than any other, this fellow was skillful in the burning of brush. Observing his methods and adding his own insights, Thoreau set down a procedure for successfully fighting fires. He also listened to the music a fire makes, roaring and crackling: "You sometimes hear it on a small scale in the log on the hearth."

Having heard the music fire makes and having discussed his fire-fighting method with one of his friends, Thoreau went farther: suggesting that along with firemen there be a band of musicians playing instruments to revive the energies of weary firemen and to cheer up those who were not yet exhausted.

Finally he said that fire is not only disadvantage. "It is without doubt an advantage on the whole. It sweeps and ventilates the forest floor, and makes it clear and clean. It is nature's broom. . . . Thus, in the course of two or three years new huckleberry fields are created for birds and for men."

Emerson said that Thoreau could have been a great leader of men, but that he ended up simply as the captain of huckleberry-picking-parties for children. But Thoreau's writing determined the actions of Martin Luther King, Jr., and Gandhi, and the Danes in their light-hearted resistance to Hitler's invasion. India. Nonviolence.

The useless tree that gave so much shade. The usefulness of the useless is good news for artists. For art serves no material purpose. It has to do with changing minds and spirits. The minds and spirits of people are changing. Not only in New York, but everywhere. It is time to give a concert of modern music in Africa. The change is not disruptive. It is cheerful.

Designed by Raymond M. Grimaila

The text was composed by P & M Typesetting, Incorporated in Linotype Caledonia with Optima display. Printing and binding by Halliday Lithograph Corporation.

Empty Words was typewritten by the author using an IBM Selectric II with two elements, Courier 12, roman and italic.

Writing for the Second Time Through Finnegans Wake was set in Monotype Bembo at the Stinehour Press. The typography was designed by Freeman Keith, the position of punctuation designed and realized by John Cage and Alison Knowles.

Except for *Preface to "Lecture on the Weather," The Future of Music,* and *Writing for the Second Time Through Finnegans Wake,* the typography was composed with the aid of I Ching chance operations.

Wesleyan University Press, Middletown, Connecticut 06457